FR. DANIEL BRANDENBURG, L.C.

◇ ◇ ◇

JOURNEY TO JOY

REFLECTIONS ON THE 7 SORROWS
OF THE BLESSED VIRGIN MARY

TABLE OF CONTENTS

FOREWORD 6

INTRODUCTION... 10
Sacred Art and Music to Aid Contemplation... 11
Reality or a Façade?... 13
Real Sorrow, Real Faith.. 14
What Is Sorrow? 18
What We See in the Seven Sorrows of Mary... 21
Personal Reflection or Discussion..22

CHAPTER 1: THE PROPHECY OF SIMEON
Sacred Music to Aid Contemplation 26
Passion, Compassion, Redemption 26
How Did Simeon's Prophecy Pierce Mary's Heart? 28
Mary's Sorrow Transformed into Joy 33
Personal Reflection or Discussion 35

CHAPTER 2: THE FLIGHT INTO EGYPT
Sacred Music to Aid Contemplation 39
Seeking Security 40
How Did the Flight into Egypt Pierce Mary's Heart?........................... 46
Mary's Sorrow Transformed into Joy 50
Personal Reflection or Discussion... 53

CHAPTER 3 THE LOSS OF JESUS IN THE TEMPLE
Sacred Music to Aid Contemplation 58
Holiness in the Humdrum 58
How Did the Loss of Jesus in the Temple Pierce Mary's Heart?........... 61
Mary's Sorrow Transformed into Joy 70
Personal Reflection or Discussion... 71

CHAPTER 4: MARY MEETS JESUS ON THE WAY TO CALVARY
Sacred Music to Aid Contemplation 76
Lose It to Find It 76
Why ... Jesus on the Way to Calvary a Sword in Mary's Heart? 77
Mary's Sorrow Transformed into Joy 87
Personal Reflection or Discussion.. 90

CHAPTER 5: JESUS DIES ON THE CROSS
Sacred Music to Aid Contemplation 93
The Proximity of Death Changes Life 94
Silence Salutes Sorrow 96
How Did Jesus' Death Pierce Mary's Heart? 98
Accompanying Jesus 100
Mary's Sorrow Transformed into Joy 106
Personal Reflection or Discussion 108

CHAPTER 6: JESUS IS PIERCED WITH A LANCE AND
LOWERED FROM THE CROSS INTO MARY'S ARMS
Sacred Music to Aid Contemplation 112
How Did This Sixth Sorrow Pierce Mary's Heart? 114
Mary's Sorrow Transformed into Joy 122
Personal Reflection or Discussion 124

CHAPTER 7: JESUS IS BURIED IN THE TOMB
Sacred Music to Aid Contemplation 127
Holding On, Letting Go 128
How Did the Burial of Christ in the Tomb Pierce Mary's Heart? 129
Mary's Sorrow Transformed into Joy 134
The Joy of the Martyrs 140
Personal Reflection or Discussion: 142

EPILOGUE
The Path 145
Obstacles in the Path 146
Gifts of the Journey 147
The Joy of the Journey 149

PRAYERS AND PROMISES 152

APPENDIX
Rosary of the Seven Sorrows 153
Promises 154
Consecration to the Sacred Heart of Jesus & Our Lady of Sorrows... 155
Novena Prayer Honoring the Seven Sorrows of Mary 156
Stabat Mater Dolorosa 158
Stabat Mater Speciosa 161
Litany of the Sacred Heart of Jesus 164

FOREWORD

When some women from Louisville, Kentucky, first approached me in 2015 about preaching a retreat to moms entitled *"Journey to Joy"* on the seven sorrows of Mary, two questions came immediately to mind.

The first question was a logical one. How can joy and sorrow go together? "Are you sure you got that title right?" I asked. After all, you usually don't find grieving widows laughing, nor newlyweds weeping. Joy and sorrow are so far removed from each other on the spectrum of human emotion that it seems illogical to stick them together in the same title.

The second question was a practical one. What are the seven sorrows? Despite years of Catholic schooling, over a decade of seminary training, and a lifetime of spiritual reading, I couldn't identify offhand what the seven sorrows of Mary were. I felt pretty ignorant.

The more I thought about the request and the title, though, the more I warmed to the idea. It struck me that I had begun my novitiate in the Legion of Christ on September 15, 1993—the day the Church celebrates Our Lady of Sorrows. I thought back to those first joyful days of consecrating my life to God and recognized that perhaps sorrow and joy were not so antithetical after all, and that I owed it to my spiritual mother to reflect more deeply on this topic.

Yes, life is hard and full of sorrow. Facing the reality of sorrow, we can either live in denial of the pain or dig deeper for meaning—and joy. Our experience of deep discomfort in life has the potential to open our horizons to deeper joys. As I reflected on this truth, the traditional devotion to the seven sorrows of Mary began to make more sense and excite my curiosity. Was the devotion a morbid, masochistic, moping on woes—or rather the confident contemplation of how to draw joy out of life's trials? Our search for meaning and our attainment of the peace and happiness we desire hinge upon our ability to journey from sorrow to joy.

That's where I began to see that a deeper reflection on Mary's seven sorrows could be triply significant.

1. I could understand my own story better. Without
    understanding your past, you cannot live your identity in the
    present or shape the future. By drawing out with greater clarity
    God's mysterious plan in linking this Catholic devotion with
    my life and the specific spirituality and history of Regnum
    Christi, I realized I could grasp his plan better.[1] We were
    originally founded in 1941 with the title "Missionaries of the
    Sacred Heart and of Our Lady of Sorrows", and from our
    earliest history we gave a special significance to that feast day
    in the Church's calendar. By delving into the seven sorrows, it
    could take on actual significance in my own life.

2. Secondly, I could help myself and others search for God's plan
    in the midst of seemingly senseless suffering. That's what the
    Virgin Mary accomplished throughout her life. Sitting at her
    feet and learning from her reveals secrets for living life better.
    Who doesn't want that? And if I could contribute in some way
    to unlock these secrets for others, to free this timeless devotion
    from pietistic exaggerations, and to couch it in more accessible
    language, it would be a great service to Catholics today.

3. Thirdly, through this contemplation, the spirituality of Regnum
    Christi might be further understood and lived out. Like most
    people's lives, including perhaps your own life, the story of
    Regnum Christi is not one of fairy tale success and human
    glory, but a history of sin, grace, and redemption. It's a history
    of God's mercy, of love that redeems, and of journeys from
    sorrow to joy. In that history, we find hope for the future.

So I decided to accept the invitation.

To prepare for the retreat series, I did what I always do: I brought it
to prayer. I take to heart the Church's injunction *contemplata aliis
tradere* (transmit what you have contemplated). On September 8, 2015,
the day the Catholic Church celebrates the joy of Mary's birthday, I
began contemplating the seven sorrows. Soon after, our Lord gave me
ample opportunities to experience firsthand what I was discovering in

---

1   The Legion of Christ is a Roman Catholic religious congregation of priests and men studying for the
     priesthood. It is part of the spiritual family of Regnum Christi. Cf. http://www.regnumchristi.org/
     en/priests/.

the life of the Virgin Mary: I had a heart attack in February of 2016 and then two years later as I was finishing the text of this book I was diagnosed with stage 3 multiple myeloma. Over the months of dialysis, chemotherapy and then bone marrow transplant, I found confirmed time and again the principles and insights that you will find in the pages of this book.

In contemplating the sorrows of Mary, I found myself immersed in the beauty of this traditional devotion, discovering what so many Christians over the centuries have found: in Mary's sorrows we find a model of faith and of how to discover joy in the midst of sorrow.

Your life has sorrows. You are meant for joy. Walk with me now as we journey from sorrow to joy.

INTRODUCTION

"Those whom the LORD has ransomed will return and enter Zion singing, crowned with everlasting joy; They will meet with joy and gladness, sorrow and mourning will flee. I, it is I who comfort you. Can you then fear mortal man, who is human only, to be looked upon as grass, and forget the LORD, your maker, who stretched out the heavens and laid the foundations of the earth?"

Isaiah 51:11–13

SACRED ART AND MUSIC TO AID CONTEMPLATION

At the beginning of each chapter of this book, I recommend various sacred songs that might help you enter more deeply into the emotions, thoughts, and joys that passed through the heart of the Blessed Virgin Mary. I have also included some Christian artwork interspersed throughout the text for the same reason. For the introduction, consider listening to these two songs:

◇ *Journey for Home* by the Consecrated Women of Regnum Christi[2]

◇ *Blessings* by Laura Story[3]

Adriaen Isenbrandt, Our Lady of the Seven Sorrows, 1518 - 1535, Church of Our Lady- Onze-Lieve-Vrouwekerk, Bruges, Belgium, https://commons. wikimedia.org/wiki/File:Adriaen_Isenbrant_-_Our_Lady_of_the_Seven_Sorrows_-_WGA11877.jpg.

---

2   This song can be found on the CD "Discovering God's Love for You" at https://store. missionnetwork.com/collections/regnum-christi-store/products/discovering-gods-love-for-you?variant=7711322931242. The original song was written by Ed Bolduc and the lyrics are available readily online.

3   https://www.youtube.com/watch?v=XQan9L3yXjc

Master of the Half Lengths, *Virgin of the Seven Sorrows*, 1530 - 1560, National Art Museum of Catalonia, Barcelona. https://www.museunacional.cat/en/colleccio/virgin-seven-sorrows/mestre-de-les-mitges-figures/008327-000.

REALITY OR A FAÇADE?

There's a lot of pressure to conform and perform in our world. You've got to *look* like you've got it all together, that you are the perfect parent, never frazzled, always in control. You've got to show that you excel at things, that you are strong, that you don't make mistakes. And this pressure is there whether or not your faith in God and religious practice are strong.

As a Catholic priest, I see so many people who live projecting an image of perfection and happiness, as if they have it all together—but I hear confessions and counsel couples, and I see behind the façade into the disordered interior of messy lives. The reality is that *everyone* struggles, everyone has their cross, and *no one* has it all together. We attempt to live behind the façade, but we all know deep down the truth about our own brokenness and misery.

I think this is why reflecting on the seven sorrows of Mary can be so liberating. She suffered. She faced setbacks. She made mistakes. The mother of God lost him in the Temple! Mary had sorrow, but she is also the greatest saint in the history of humanity. She didn't live a life without difficulties, nor did she run away from problems. She "kept all these things in her heart" (Luke 2:51) and through prayer found the purpose and meaning of all things.

To reflect on Mary's sorrows is to peel back the mask that we wear, to drop the false façade of perfection, and to open up our horizons to the deep truth that holiness doesn't come from us holding it all together, but from God holding us. His grace and mercy are the defining point of a truly Christian life.

If you continue trying to live behind your façade, with false expectations about yourself and life, you'll never be truly happy or at peace. You will always feel your inadequacy, that you can never be good enough. We can try to hide our sorrows and pain, but they will eventually seep out. All the resentment, bitterness, unforgiveness, neglect, abuse, and fear that we have experienced in our lives are the source of our sorrows, and they are not healed simply by the passing of time. Only by facing them as the Blessed Virgin Mary did will we be healed. By latching onto God's grace and mercy, we can be freed. By knowing Jesus Christ as his mother does, we can know joy.

REAL SORROW, REAL FAITH

Sorrow has the potential to lead us to deeper faith.

I recently spoke with a mom who was the model Catholic woman. Let's call her Cheryl. She'd graduated with a psychology degree from a prestigious Catholic university, raised many talented and well-behaved kids, and had a loving husband. Cheryl was active in her parish and school, well respected, and always helping others.

A diagnosis of thyroid cancer shook her idyllic world.

Her initial reaction of surprise and shock quickly gave way to anger. "How could God let this happen to my family? What did I do wrong? Why me?"

Cheryl was experiencing in her own flesh what the *Catechism of the Catholic Church* says in number 164: "The world we live in often seems very far from the one promised us by faith. Our experiences of evil and suffering, injustice and death, seem to contradict the Good News; they can shake our faith and become a temptation against it."

When friends found out, they reached out with condolences, offers to bring meals, and promises of prayer. But Cheryl was angry. She didn't want those things; she wanted her health and pleasant life back. In a fiery Facebook post, she told people to keep their pious platitudes to themselves, and that she didn't want anyone visiting or asking her how she was doing.

Where was Cheryl's faith? What happened to the perfect Catholic mom? Had a few cancer cells killed her convictions?

YouCat number 51 transforms Cheryl's and every suffering person's question.

> *The decisive question is therefore not, "How can anyone believe in a good God when there is so much evil?" but rather, "How could a person with a heart and understanding endure life in this world if God did not exist?" Christ's death and Resurrection show us that evil did not have the first word, nor does it have*

the last. God made absolute good result from the worst evil. We believe that in the Last Judgment God will put an end to all injustice. In the life of the world to come, evil no longer has any place and suffering ends.

It wasn't that Cheryl's faith was gone, but it was being challenged. That's not a bad thing. God likes to stretch us, because it is only when we go beyond our comfort zone that we can mature and develop. If a bodybuilder only lifted weights that were comfortable, his muscles would stay puny. How can we expect our faith to grow if we just stay comfortable?

It is precisely when our faith is tested that we have the chance to broaden our horizons and realize that there is something more, something better. I know that happened in Cheryl's life; she overcame the illness and grew tremendously in faith. It certainly happened in my life.

Around February 2009, I broke my wrist in a snowboarding accident and had to go to the hospital. The break was a serious one, and the doctor's prognosis was that I would be in a cast for 3 months without regaining full mobility for four or five months. I get antsy when I can't exercise or play sports, and my ministry at that point depended greatly on my ability to type, so this was a very inconvenient problem. Plus, I was in a lot of pain.

So, I was not in a good mood at all after the doctor's words, and while walking from his office to another hospital office to fill out paperwork, I was interiorly grumbling, "God, why did you permit this? Can't you see that I'm trying to do your work? Why now?"

Three women were working in that next office. They saw me walk in, dressed in black and wearing a Roman collar. After a couple of initial questions to fill out my paperwork, the conversation shifted. "I've always wanted to ask a priest," said Sarah, a Protestant. "Why do you Catholics go to confession?" After I explained to her the scriptural basis and great graces that come from this sacrament, Sarah turned to her closet Catholic colleague in the office and asked, "Mary, how long has it been since you last went to confession?"

Up to that point, Mary had shown interest in the conversation, but at Sarah's sudden question, she turned red, looked down, and mumbled something indistinct under her breath. "What was that?" I asked. "Eighteen years" she whispered reluctantly. "Wow, that's a long time!" exclaimed Sarah. I couldn't help quipping, "I guess it's high time for another confession! When's the next time you'll have a priest walk into your office?" Mary said no thanks, so I let it rest. As the conversation continued, Mary explained why she had not been to confession for so many years. The story had to do with her son. Eighteen years ago, her rambunctious boy had gotten himself kicked out of Catholic school. A young mother at the time, Mary felt mistreated, so she left the Catholic Church. It turned out that her son's birthday would have been two days before I appeared on the scene, but he had died just a few months before in a fatal car accident. Upon hearing this news, I offered to pray for him and celebrate a Mass for the repose of his soul.

"Thank you," said Mary, tears forming in her eyes.

"What was his name, so I can pray for him?" I asked.

"His name was Daniel," she said.

I gave her a funny look. "You're kidding!" I said. "That's my name!"

"His full name was Daniel Brae Rosenberger," she said.

I just looked at her and said, "My name is Daniel Brandenburg." By now, her tears were flowing.

"Mary, this is too much of a coincidence," I said. "I think God is really speaking to your heart right now. This is a moment of grace. Are you sure you don't want to go to confession?"

She stood there, wavering. At that moment, Sarah piped up to the third lady who had been typing away quietly in the corner, "You know, I think it's high time for our coffee break! You two take care of what you need to take care of. We'll be back in a little while." And without missing a beat, the two women got up and left the room.

Mary was sobbing, so we talked a little more. Once she had calmed down a bit, I offered again to hear her confession and she said yes. So, I listened to her sins and guilt and pain, gave her absolution, and welcomed her back to the Church after eighteen years away. It had truly been a day of grace for Mary. As I left her office, I was kicking myself as I prayed, "Lord, if this is what it takes to bring a person back to the Church after 18 years, then take the other wrist too!"

I was reminded that day how God can bring so much good out of suffering. The deepest pains in life can lead to the deepest joys. "God whispers in our joys; he speaks in our conscience. But in our sorrows he shouts. They are the megaphone with which he awakens a deaf world."[4] By contemplating the seven sorrows of Mary, our faith grows, and the world awakens.

---

4   C.S. Lewis. As quoted in *YouCat*, in the margin next to question 52.

WHAT IS SORROW?

We all know intuitively what sorrow is. As St. Thomas Aquinas says, it is the emotion, feeling, or passion that we feel in the face of present evil (or absence of good).[5] The deeper the evil, the more profound our reaction to it. At a more superficial level of evil, we might experience disappointment. Like when a flight is delayed, or a spouse comes home late from work, we can be irked or disappointed... but I wouldn't say that it is a sorrow. But as evil touches us more deeply, we move from disappointment to sadness to sorrow. If a friend lets you down, you'll be sad; if your friend betrays you, you'll experience sorrow. The deepest wounds are sorrows.

By itself, the feeling of sorrow is not morally good or bad. It just is. We experience it. It is a normal human reaction to the presence of evil or absence of good in our lives. It is a passion, and as such is morally neutral. How we freely respond to that sorrow is where our freedom comes into play, and hence our moral goodness or badness.

St. Thomas Aquinas states that, "The perfection of moral virtue does not wholly take away the passions, but regulates them."[6] This means that the passions—sorrow included—need to be channeled and governed by our reason and by good habits (i.e. virtues) that we develop.[7] On the flip side, the passions can also be derailed and perverted by bad habits. So how do we ensure that virtue rules over emotions, and that we don't become a slave to passions through bad habits?

This is not simply a question of willpower, though that is also important. I could have a strong will to keep my diet and not gobble up every piece of chocolate cake that I see, but I first need to assent intellectually to the idea that the diet is a good thing. If I don't, my will won't work. After all, chocolate cake is good and desirable—so

---

5   St. Thomas Aquinas, *Summa Theologiae*, I–II, q.22. St. Thomas has a comprehensive presentation of these emotions or passions, demonstrating that they are present in our sensitive appetite (i.e. our desire for good and aversion to evil), either approaching what is good or withdrawing from what is evil. He explains why there are 11 passions, and most of them in contrary pairs: *love* and *hatred*, *desire* and *aversion*, *joy* and *sorrow* for the concupiscible appetite (i.e., sensible good or evil), *hope* and *despair*, *daring* and *fear*, plus *anger* that has no pair within the irascible appetite (i.e. good or evil that isn't easy).

6   St. Thomas Aquinas, *Summa Theologiae*, I, q.95, a.2, ad.3.

7   Cf. *Catechism of the Catholic Church*, n.1762-1774.

there must be something better and more desirable that keeps me
from gluttony. It is the mind that directs the will to the more desirable
good, and the will's experience of goodness strengthens the mind's
appreciation. That is why regulating our passions begins with our
mind. Its part in setting the passions straight can be done in three ways:

1. *Correcting our misapprehension of reality.* Sometimes, we get
    mixed up in our perception of things. Perhaps I thought my son
    was lying to me, so I was angry, but it turns out he actually was
    telling the truth. Once I realize my mistake, my anger subsides
    and turns into remorse for thinking the worst. That's when I
    can apologize and move on. It was a simple mistake.

2. *Correcting our value system (i.e. what is good or evil).* This
    is a bit trickier. Sometimes, our values don't correspond to
    reality and to the way God sees things. For example, someone
    may have reasoned that abortion is a good thing for choice and
    freedom, and so when they see that a woman cannot get an
    abortion due to laws or lack of access, they might experience
    sorrow over that lack of "opportunity" and anger because of
    the "injustice." Until their value system changes, the passions
    they experience won't change. Those passions, perverted by
    vice and erroneous opinion, will reinforce the flawed value
    system. That system will change only through a deeper
    personal experience of reality or argumentation that opens
    them to the truth. Exposure to fresh ideas and perspectives,
    contact with the teachings of the Church, or time spend with
    Scripture can often help, but it is primarily the existential
    experience that achieves the adjustment of values. We can see
    this at work in Abby Johnson, a former worker at a Planned
    Parenthood clinic whose firsthand experience of the brutality
    and brokenness of abortion led her to abandon the business
    and faulty value system that upheld it. Correcting our value
    system is hard, because it requires humility, openness to the
    truth, and docility to it. But the truth also sets us free.

3. *Broadening our vision and values.* A person might think that
    the pleasure of food or sex, the praise of the crowds, or the
    power trip of authority are the greatest goods of life, simply
    because they haven't yet experienced the deeper joys of selfless

love, the peace of contemplation, or the promise of eternal life. Good books and conversation with good people can open our horizons to so much more. There are many things that are not immediately apparent to us, but are nonetheless part of reality. A mother who grieves the death of her soldier son can open her heart to rejoice in the lives saved by him jumping on the grenade. True open-mindedness can lead us to value what before we saw as unbearable. Faith is the greatest spur to open-mindedness, because through it entirely new dimensions are opened. Faith constantly opens us to the truth that sets us free.

Reflecting on the seven sorrows of Mary can help us to modulate our passions in these three ways, rounding out our Christian personality and introducing us to a greater spiritual freedom.

WHAT WE SEE IN THE SEVEN SORROWS OF MARY

Just what are the sorrows of Mary? Tradition has handed down seven primary sorrows:

1. The prophecy of Simeon

2. The flight into Egypt

3. The loss of Jesus in the Temple

4. Mary meets Jesus on the way to Calvary

5. Jesus dies on the Cross

6. Jesus is pierced with a lance and placed in Mary's arms

7. Jesus is buried in the tomb

Three of Mary's sorrows relate to Jesus's his early life and childhood, while the last four relate to his crucifixion and death. True Marian devotion is always Christ-centered, just as we see here with the seven sorrows. The Mother of God draws grace in her life from Jesus, and she always draws us to Jesus, not to herself. Mary leads us to her Son.

All of these sorrows of Mary share three characteristics.

1. Each one is related to our experience of life. They are not distant mythological or abstract theological reflections. They are real. They are relatable. They touch on our life experience. Because we can recognize our own life in Mary's sorrows, her manner of dealing with those sorrows can directly affect our life. While we might accept in faith that there are three persons in the Trinity, or that Jesus is true God and true man, those don't touch us quite as much as a mother looking plaintively into our eyes as she holds the bloodied corpse of her son. Mary's sorrows are real, to the point of being shocking.

2. Secondly, each of Mary's sorrows stems from her relationship with Jesus. If she didn't love, she wouldn't have suffered. Love does that. It brings both sorrow and joy. The more you love someone, the deeper the wound when they are absent or when they let you down. We suffer because we love. And if we choose not to love, we suffer even more, because we truncate the deep human need not to live in isolation, but to live loving and being loved. Mary's love for her Son is deep, real, and total. That's why her sorrows are so poignant. She models for us how to love Jesus and how to handle the sorrows that will inevitably present themselves in our lives.

3. Thirdly, none of the seven sorrows end in sorrow. Each one is transformed into deeper faith, deeper joy. That's exciting! That is hope-filled! A way to transform sadness to gladness? That is revolutionary! Discovering Mary's method for converting sorrow to joy may just be the single most important step in your own spiritual life.

For those who have their life together already, there's no reason to waste time with this book. They are already there. But for anyone who wants to journey from sorrow to joy, let's walk together and sneak a peek into the heart of the Blessed Virgin Mary.

QUESTIONS FOR PERSONAL REFLECTION OR DISCUSSION

1. What kind of pressure do I feel to conform or perform? Do I feel like I've got it all together?

2. Pelagianism was one of the first heresies the Catholic Church had to face. It affirmed that we could become perfect and holy by our own effort, without God's grace. Have I found myself trying to be perfect so that I can be worthy of God's love? How so? Or do I truly trust in the gratuitous, unconditional love of God, our Father who is rich in mercy?

3. How have sorrows in my life helped me to turn more fully to God and rely on his grace? How have sorrows helped to "awaken the world," in the words of C.S. Lewis?

4. Am I aware that I could channel and regulate my emotions, feelings, and passions? Do I see a need to rectify anything in my comprehension, value system, or openness of mind?

5. What are some ways that I have shown true compassion to others? What are some ways that I have recognized the redemptive value of my suffering?

6. Which of the seven sorrows catches my attention most at first glance? Why?

CHAPTER 1

THE PROPHECY
OF SIMEON

"You are anxious and worried about many things. There is need of only one
thing. Mary has chosen the better part and it will not be taken from her."
Luke 10:41–42

Benjamin West, *Simeon with the Infant Jesus*, ca. 1796, Flint Institute of Arts, Flint, MI. https://flintarts.
org/art/objects/420.

SACRED MUSIC TO AID CONTEMPLATION

◇   *Mary Did You Know* by Pentatonix[8]

◇   *Child of the Poor* by the Consecrated Women of
      Regnum Christi[9]

PASSION, COMPASSION, REDEMPTION

In the introductory chapter, we began to understand a little bit better
what sorrow is. It is a passion, that is, something that happens to us
and that elicits a spontaneous emotional response. The passion of
sorrow arises naturally within us when we experience an evil that is
present (or a good that is absent). It is deeper than disappointment or
simple sadness; sorrow arises when our deepest desires are not met.
Passions need to be guided by virtue, and sometimes corrected and
transformed.

In the traditional devotion of the seven sorrows of the Blessed Virgin
Mary, she shows us the way to change sorrow into joy. As we begin
now to take a closer look at her sorrows, we will consistently see three
ways that she elevates her gaze to a higher plane, transforming that
sorrow into joy:

1.   *Sorrow is a passion.* Sadness, suffering, and sorrow are an
      inescapable part of our human experience. The emotion or
      passion (from Latin *passio*, "suffering") is morally neutral.
      How we freely react to what we suffer makes us good or bad.
      Faced with the experience of suffering, Mary responds with
      faith, trust in God, forbearance, and many other virtues. In
      each of our reflections on a sorrow of Mary, we'll see more
      closely how her attitudes and responses to what she suffers
      make her holy. She is not holy because she doesn't experience
      difficulties, but because of how she handles them. She is never
      a victim bemoaning her plight or making excuses. She suffers
      more than any woman ever did, yet never makes her sufferings
      the center of her life. She is more than her sorrows.

8   https://www.youtube.com/watch?v=ifCWN5pJGIE

9   Available on iTunes at https://itunes.apple.com/us/album/emmanuel-god-with-us/775010900 or
      CDBaby https://store.cdbaby.com/cd/consecratedwomenofregnum2.

2. *Sorrow for another is compassion.* Real nobility of soul is shown when one's heart has space for others. We must resist two extremes: on the one hand, the activist tendency to simply fix problems, without first feeling the pain of our neighbors and accompanying them in their sorrow; and on the other hand, the pity-party tendency to wail with the widow, without lifting a finger to practically alleviate her suffering.[10] True compassion leads us not merely to commiserate with others, but also to rectify or remove the evil in their lives, inasmuch as we are able to do so. The Blessed Virgin Mary shows us throughout her sorrows how to make room in our hearts for the suffering of others, how to show true compassion.

3. *Sorrow borne for and with Christ is redemptive.* A person can endure any "what" if they have a "why." Through faith, we can see the "why" of our suffering, and unite it with the suffering of Jesus. That's what Mary does throughout her life. That is what we discover and begin to understand when we reflect on her seven sorrows. The first reading for Mass on the memorial of Our Lady of Sorrows is taken from 1 Peter 4:13: "But rejoice to the extent that you share in the sufferings of Christ, so that when his glory is revealed you may also rejoice exultantly." Truly, suffering and sorrow can become the source of our joy.

---

10   James 2:15–16 "If a brother or sister has nothing to wear and has no food for the day, and one of you says to them, 'Go in peace, keep warm, and eat well,' but you do not give them the necessities of the body, what good is it?"

HOW DID SIMEON'S PROPHECY PIERCE MARY'S HEART?

To understand why Simeon's prophecy was Mary's first sorrow, we need to understand what was going on in her life. It had been a tough year for her even before Simeon came on the scene. She'd been frightened by the appearance of an angel with a cryptic announcement that puts her into an awkward bind with Joseph: Gabriel neglected to appear to him and let him in on the plan. And that plan hadn't been so clear in the first place, and even her question to the angel about how this was all going to work out didn't elicit much more detail.

Sometimes we mistakenly think that Mary received perfect foreknowledge from God, that somehow she had a fully detailed script of what was going to happen in her life. After all, wasn't she the Immaculate Conception, "full of grace," and Mother of God?

Yes, she was all that, but that didn't give her divine omniscience. The Virgin Mary is blessed because she believed,[11] not because she saw or knew everything beforehand. And if we believe as she did, we too will be blessed. Her faith led her to silence, prayer, and a desire for quiet contemplation. She "kept all these things, reflecting on them in her heart" (Luke 2:19). The Blessed Virgin Mary:

> is continually involved in mysteries the sense and meaning of which tower over her, but instead of resigning herself to bafflement she gives them space in her heart in order to continually mull over them there (the Greek word Luke uses at 2:19, symballein, really means to throw together, to compare and hence to consider from all possible angles). This means that in no way at all does she understand everything completely from the first moment onward but has to work away tirelessly in order to understand all these overpowering ideas as well as she may.[12]

---

11   Luke 11:27-28 "While he was speaking, a woman from the crowd called out and said to him, 'Blessed is the womb that carried you and the breasts at which you nursed.' He replied, 'Rather, blessed are those who hear the word of God and observe it.' "

12   Hans Urs Von Balthasar, *Mary for Today*, Ignatius Press, 1988, p. 36.

Mary trusts. She knows that God would not deceive, mislead, or abandon her. And as the child grew within her, she must have experienced such profound joy. Not understanding everything, but yes—knowing that God is with her, that God is *within* her, that God is with us (that's the meaning of the word "Emmanuel"). What intimate moments she must have had! A daily increasing awareness of the mystery of God's salvation. And then Joseph has his dream and takes her into his home, removing any shade of worry about being abandoned or stoned. Things are going so well. Even the surprise census from Caesar Augustus forcing them to travel to Bethlehem in her last weeks of pregnancy works out fine in the end. And at the birth of her son, despite the lowly surroundings all is raised to mysterious heights as angels are seen by the shepherds who bring the glad tidings to Mary, and by the Magi who bring gifts fit for a king. Yes, things have been going so well! And that is why she "kept all these things, reflecting on them in her heart" (Luke 2:19).

It's in this joyful context of an almost fairy tale idyll that Simeon comes onto the scene. Everything is going according to plan. As the Gospel of Luke relates,

> *When eight days were completed for his circumcision,*
> *he was named Jesus, the name given him by the angel*
> *before he was conceived in the womb. When the days*
> *were completed for their purification according to*
> *the law of Moses, they took him up to Jerusalem to*
> *present him to the Lord, just as it is written in the law*
> *of the Lord, 'Every male that opens the womb shall*
> *be consecrated to the Lord,' and to offer the sacrifice*
> *of 'a pair of turtledoves or two young pigeons,' in*
> *accordance with the dictate in the law of the Lord.*
> *Luke 2:21–24*

Note how Luke highlights that Mary and Joseph did everything "according to the law of Moses" and "in accordance with the dictate in the law of the Lord." They were so conscientious. Trying to do everything right.

Until now, Mary had handled the setbacks in her life with great
confidence in God's protection. But now God throws her a curveball. In
comes Simeon:

> Now there was a man in Jerusalem whose name was
> Simeon. This man was righteous and devout, awaiting
> the consolation of Israel, and the holy Spirit was upon
> him. It had been revealed to him by the holy Spirit that
> he should not see death before he had seen the Messiah
> of the Lord. He came in the Spirit into the temple....
> Luke 2:25–27

Scripture makes it clear that Simeon is a man of God. He has received a
special promise, a singular grace: to see the Messiah before he dies. And
he is led by the Holy Spirit, the same Spirit that overshadowed Mary
and initiated God's plan in her life.

> ....And when the parents brought in the child Jesus
> to perform the custom of the law in regard to him, he
> took him into his arms and blessed God."
> Luke 2:27–28

Mary is a first-time mother. Having a total stranger walk up and take
her baby away must have caused some consternation. "Who is this guy?
Does he know how to hold a baby?" And as the crinkly old man reaches
for Jesus, Mary must have cringed a bit, and as Simeon lifts him, at
least thought "Careful with his head! Don't drop him!"

A broad smile breaks across the wizened face of Simeon as his life
dream is realized. His elated words of fulfillment ring out in praise of
God:

> Now, Master, you may let your servant go in peace,
> according to your word, for my eyes have seen your
> salvation, which you prepared in sight of all the
> peoples, a light for revelation to the Gentiles, and glory
> for your people Israel.
> Luke 2:29–32

These words strike a chord in Mary's heart. Yes, as a mother she's
anxious for her child, but as an Israelite she's anxious for her people.

And Simeon is saying something that links them. Yes, even confirming what the angel had said. The Messiah! The glory of our people. Yes, her son was something special. The pride surging up in her breast as her son is praised wipes away the worry. "Sure, this old guy can hold him! If he keeps talking like this, he can hold him all day." Don't you love to hear praises heaped upon your children? Few things warm a mother's heart more than accolades for their offspring.

Yet this is where the sorrow begins. The more we love, the greater our vulnerability to sorrow. Sorrow, though, is not opposed to joy; in fact, the deepest joys often come together with sorrow:

◇ In childbirth, the intense physical pain is overshadowed by the joy of new life.[13]

◇ In marriage, the sorrow of separation from family and loss of possibilities dissipates with the joy of spousal love and the start of a new family.[14]

◇ In death, the sorrow of a lost loved one is dulled by relief that their suffering in this life has ended, and hope in the promise of an eternal life better beyond belief.[15]

Then come the ambivalent words of Simeon's prophecy:

> The child's father and mother were amazed at what was said about him; and Simeon blessed them and said to Mary his mother, "Behold, this child is destined for the fall and rise of many in Israel, and to be a sign that will be contradicted (and you yourself a sword will pierce) so that the thoughts of many hearts may be revealed."
> Luke 2:33–35

---

13   Cf. John 16:21 "When a woman is in labor, she is in anguish because her hour has arrived; but when she has given birth to a child, she no longer remembers the pain because of her joy that a child has been born into the world."

14   Cf. Tobit 11:17 "Before them all Tobit proclaimed how God had shown mercy to him and opened his eyes. When Tobit came up to Sarah, the wife of his son Tobiah, he blessed her and said: 'Welcome, my daughter! Blessed be your God for bringing you to us, daughter! Blessed are your father and your mother. Blessed be my son Tobiah, and blessed be you, daughter! Welcome to your home with blessing and joy. Come in, daughter!' That day there was joy for all the Jews who lived in Nineveh."

15   Philippians 1:20–21 "My eager expectation and hope is that I shall not be put to shame in any way, but that with all boldness, now as always, Christ will be magnified in my body, whether by life or by death. For to me life is Christ, and death is gain."

A troubled look crosses Mary's brow. How should she understand this? On the one hand the rise and fall—clearly a sign of his greatness, the impact he'll have on the world—but on the other hand contradiction and a sword. Clouds of doubt swirl through her mind and heart. A sword? Violence? Contradiction implies controversy, rejection, conflict. Isn't he supposed to be the Prince of Peace? Why me? Why my son?

Simeon's simple words threaten the peace that had reigned in her heart. His open-ended prediction leaves room for all sorts of suppositions and worst-case scenarios to play out in her mind. Her acute intelligence begins to imagine the worst, to stir up worry.

Worry. That fear of what evil the future might bring. Worry. How it can steal our peace and roil our hearts! We all experience it. "Will people like me?" "When will the next terrorist attack come?" "Will I keep my job?" "What will happen to my children?" "Will I have enough to live on during my retirement?"

Worry. It comes about from a combination of love and uncertainty. We desire something good, but don't know whether we can attain it or keep it in the face of dangers or opposition from all around. Worry. It steals our peace and serenity.

We know what Jesus says about worry.

> *Therefore, I tell you, do not worry about your life, what you will eat (or drink), or about your body, what you will wear. Is not life more than food and the body more than clothing? Look at the birds in the sky; they do not sow or reap, they gather nothing into barns, yet your heavenly Father feeds them. Are not you more important than they? Can any of you by worrying add a single moment to your life-span? Why are you anxious about clothes? Learn from the way the wildflowers grow. They do not work or spin. But I tell you that not even Solomon in all his splendor was clothed like one of them. If God so clothes the grass of the field, which grows today and is thrown into the oven tomorrow, will he not much more provide for you, O you of little faith? So, do not worry and say, 'What are we to*

eat?' or 'What are we to drink?' or 'What are we to
wear?' All these things the pagans seek. Your heavenly
Father knows that you need them all. But seek first the
kingdom (of God) and his righteousness, and all these
things will be given you besides. Do not worry about
tomorrow; tomorrow will take care of itself. Sufficient
for a day is its own evil.
Matthew 6:25–34

Worry doesn't come from God. It comes from our own insecurity, from seeing reality in an incomplete way. It comes from focusing on the wrong things.

The Lord said to her in reply, "Martha, Martha, you
are anxious and worried about many things. There
is need of only one thing. Mary has chosen the better
part and it will not be taken from her."
Luke 10:41–42

MARY'S SORROW TRANSFORMED INTO JOY

The better part that Christ wants for you is peace, serenity, fulfillment, and joy. Not worry. Not fear. Not insecurity, bitterness, or dread.

The Virgin Mary experienced the temptation to worry just as we do. But she didn't let worry rule her and take away the better part. She kept her heart focused on the Kingdom of God. Her response teaches us how to handle setbacks in our own life. The way she overcame worry is the same way that—with God's grace—you, too, can not merely minimize, but actually eliminate worry in your life. Wouldn't that be amazing! What did Mary do? In the Magnificat (Luke 1:46–55) we see three simple things that she does:

1. *Live in the present.* Worry makes us live the *possible* evil of the future in the present. That's silly. It's not here for real. While we can make provision for the future, there's no sense worrying about it. "Sufficient for a day is its own evil" says our Lord (Mt 6:34). Mary "proclaims the greatness of the Lord" and "rejoices in God my Savior" (Luke 1:46–47). These verbs are

in the present tense because she is choosing to live in the reality of the present moment, in the *now* of God's presence and goodness. That soothes her soul and brings peace despite the difficulties surrounding her.

2. *Reflect on the past.* In her prayer the Magnificat, she harkens back to the history of her people, seeing the constant loving presence of the Lord who chose them, who never abandoned them, who "remembered his promise of mercy" (Luke 1:54). When they had separated themselves from their God, penance and purification brought them back. She experiences this in her own life also. Banking on her experience and the wisdom derived from her people's past in the Scriptures, it is clear that God's grace has sustained them, and will going forward.

3. *Trust in God's Providence.* Mary's hymn of praise looks toward the future ("From this day all generations will call me blessed") and embraces the promises of the Lord ("the promise he made to our fathers, to Abraham and his children forever"). Reflection on the past gives her confidence for the future. Watch small children. When they are frightened, they will run to their mom or dad, grab their legs to hide behind, or clamber into their arms. There they feel safe. What is true for children is true for adults. The future cannot cause us to worry when we know we are in the arms of a loving Father. That's why the Divine Mercy prayer—"Jesus, I trust in you!"—is so powerful. When worry threatens to take hold, repeat that simple prayer. "Jesus, I trust in you!" As Mary does, in God's Providence we will find security and peace.

As Simeon pronounced his prophecy, the Virgin Mary was tempted to worry, but instead she chose the better part. By reflecting on the past, she derived the wisdom to see God's loving care; by living in the present, she chose to live in the reality of God's goodness; by trusting in God's Providence, she set aside all worry. "Do not let your hearts be troubled. You have faith in God; have faith also in me," says our Lord in John 14:1.

By faith, Mary transforms her anxiety and worries into a deeper union with her Son and a greater confidence in God's Providence. With her help, we can do the same. There is no worry that cannot be dissipated by God's grace and a deeper trust in Him. "Jesus, I trust in you!"

The Blessed Virgin Mary was intimately united with the Holy Spirit from the moment of the Incarnation. That's why her reactions to the seven sorrows reveal how the seven gifts of the Holy Spirit work.[16] Her trust in God—despite the temptations to anxiety and worry—show true wisdom and help put everything into perspective and to not sweat the small stuff—and even the big stuff.

Let's take a few moments to look into our own hearts and see if there are attitudes that need to change. God wants you to live in the fruits of the Holy Spirit[17], in his joy and peace. Only by living as Mary did, rooted in faith, hope, and love, can we be freed from the stress, anxiety, and worry that steal our peace. Let's reflect and pray now.

QUESTIONS FOR PERSONAL REFLECTION OR DISCUSSION

1. What do I find myself worrying about? How do I bring those worries to Jesus in faith?

2. Have I learned to trust in God's Providence in a way that dissipates worry, because I recognize in faith that as my loving Father he will never let anything separate me from him? Do I feel that he holds me in his arms? In what ways have I separated myself from him?

3. In what ways do I seek control in my life? Do I trust God enough to relinquish everything to him? How can I grow in trust?

---

16   The Catechism of the Catholic Church describes these gifts in number 1831: "The seven gifts of the Holy Spirit are wisdom, understanding, counsel, fortitude, knowledge, piety, and fear of the Lord. They belong in their fullness to Christ, Son of David. They complete and perfect the virtues of those who receive them. They make the faithful docile in readily obeying divine inspirations." These gifts should not be confused with the gifts of the Holy Spirit often referenced in the Charismatic Renewal such as prophecy, speaking in tongues, etc. St. Thomas Aquinas in the Summa Theologiae, I-II, q.68 describes in a masterful way how to understand the gifts of the Holy Spirit in relation to the theological (faith, hope, love) and moral virtues (prudence, justice, fortitude, temperance). He defines the gifts as "habits perfecting man so that he is ready to follow the promptings of the Holy Spirit."

17   Galatians 5:22-23. "The fruit of the Spirit is love, joy, peace, forbearance, kindness, goodness, faithfulness, gentleness, and self-control."

4. When I experience worry, do I get so caught up in the present concerns that I lose sight of how God has cared for me in the past? Or of how his Divine Providence provides for the future?

5. Do I live mired in the sins of my past, without trusting in God's mercy? Have I sought out the freedom that God wants to give me in the sacrament of Reconciliation?

6. Do I see wisdom, the gift of the Holy Spirit, present in my life? Does that wisdom help me to put everything in perspective and keep my peace, even amid trials? Have I asked for this gift in prayer?

AN INVITATION TO PRAYER

Dear Mother of God, your life was never free from the temptation to worry. From the angel Gabriel's announcement until the end of your earthly pilgrimage, so much more remained unknown than known. With Simeon's prophecy of contradiction for your Son and a sword for you, the whirling winds of worry threatened to steal your peace. But in all of this, you recalled the words of the Psalmist, "When I am filled with cares, your comfort brings me joy" (Ps 94:19). You kept your heart and mind fixed on the Lord's faithful love to his people in the past, his guiding presence in the present, and his Divine Providence watching over the future. Blessed are you, Mary, because you believed! O Blessed Virgin Mary, teach me to trust! In the midst of my sorrows and anxieties, help me to find the peace of Christ that surpasses all understanding. By believing and trusting in the Lord as you did, I know that my life, too, will be blessed. Bring me, sweet Mother, to my eternal home.

Hail Mary, full of grace...

Jesus, I trust in you!

CHAPTER 2

THE FLIGHT INTO EGYPT

"When Israel was a child I loved him, out of Egypt I called my son."
Hosea 11:1

"He stayed there until the death of Herod, that what the Lord had said
through the prophet might be fulfilled, 'Out of Egypt I called my son.'"
Matthew 2:15

SACRED MUSIC TO AID CONTEMPLATION

◇ *Through the Desert* by the Consecrated Women of
   Regnum Christi[18]

◇ *I Shall Not Want* by Audrey Assad[19]

◇ *Sicut Cervus* by Richard Proulx[20]

Unknown artist, *The Holy Family's Flight into Egypt*, https://wau.org/resources/article/the_holy_familys_
flight_into_egypt/.

---

18   Available on the album "Nothing More Real" at https://store.cdbaby.com/cd/
     consecratedwomenofregnum.

19   https://www.youtube.com/watch?v=r8Td9cZajyE

20   https://www.youtube.com/watch?v=luc71pEHMsY

SEEKING SECURITY

Security is one of our deepest human instincts. We all desire to be comfortable, well-situated, safe, and warm. That's why we build homes and don't simply live outside and wear clothing to adjust to the climate. (Though if it weren't for women, I think men might just do that!) We protect ourselves and our homes with lighting, safety outlets, and security systems. Someone recently told me about the four simple parts of the Arkansas home security system:

1. Go to a flea market and buy an old pair of men's size 14–16 boots.

2. Place them on your front porch, along with a copy of *Guns & Ammo* magazine.

3. Put three giant dog food dishes next to the boots and magazine.

4. Leave a note on the front door that reads: *"Bubba, me and Marcel, Billy, and Jimmy Earl went for more ammo and beer. Be back in an hour. Don't mess with the pit bulls. They got the mailman this morning and messed him up bad. I don't think Killer took part, but it was hard to tell from all the blood. Anyway, I locked the three of 'em in the house. Better wait outside. Be right back. Cooter."*

We can joke, but we all know that a home is more than just a functional reality. It is (or should be) a safe haven, and from that position of safety, we can feel secure, and we can thrive. From there, we can set off on new adventures. But if we lack a home or haven—physically, emotionally, or spiritually—fear and uncertainty will reign, and our human existence will be much more difficult.

So where can we search for this security? Where do we entrust our hearts?

I cannot answer that question for you, but I can point out some sand that won't withstand the rains of life. If you want to build your foundation on rock, avoid the three Ps.

The first P is pleasure. It is tied to the root vice of sensuality and it is placing our confidence in things. Things can never ever provide us the

IDOLS	ROOT VICE	CONFIDENCE IN...	MANIFESTATIONS	QUICK TEST
PLEASURE & POSSESSIONS	Sensuality	Things	Seeking comfort (food, sex, rest)	Do I lose peace when I see that evaporate? *St. Lawrence and the Treasures of the Church*
POSITION	Vanity	Others	Social position, esteem of others, positions in the Church	Do I lose peace when I am misunderstood or overlooked? *St. Therese as the Toy in the Corner*
POWER	Pride	Self	Self-Sufficiency, Independent Streak, Don't Need Others, I'll Change Myself	Do I lose peace when I am misunderstood or overlooked? *Fr. Walter Ciszek*

security we seek. I recently rode with a man on the MARTA—Atlanta's mass transit system—who'd had a seventy-hour work week, a five-bedroom house, three BMWs, and all the other toys to go along with his high-flying lifestyle. But he was unhappy, and one day he sat down and realized how much he was spending on insurance and security systems to protect all this stuff that wasn't making him happy anyway. He decided to downsize and simplify based on a book on modern minimalism he had read. It's funny how present-day wisdom always seems to come around to what the Catholic Church discovered long ago. Pleasure and stuff can never fill the deepest desires of our hearts.

The second P is position. This is tied to the root vice of vanity: placing our confidence and security in other people, what others think about us, our social standing or recognition in the workplace, or the praise we receive (or don't). We know that's a very shaky foundation, because it rests on the fallible opinions and whims of other people. "Cursed is the man who places his trust in man" says Scripture (Jer 17:5). We have all experienced that.

The third P that cannot provide a solid foundation for our security is power. It comes from the root vice of pride, placing our confidence in ourselves. The problem is that "God resists the proud" (Prv 16:5 and Jas 4:6) and pride is the source of strife, division, and ultimate failure (cf. Is 23:9; Prv 8:13, 11:2, 13:10, 16:18, 21:4; Ps 10:4; Rom 12:16; Jas 4:6; Luke 1:46–55). On the contrary, God raises the humble - like the Blessed Virgin Mary - to honor and ultimate victory.

The three Ps are sand. They wash away in the storms of life (cf. Mt 7:24–27). And how can you tell if perhaps you are living in one of those Ps? Well, look at what is going on in your life, how you act and react. If you are placing your confidence and your security in things, you might see that manifested in overindulging in food or looking for new toys, whether they are gadgets or cars; the newest clothing or styles or fashion; or money, jobs, investments, assets, securities—all those financial things. None of those can provide the security the heart seeks, but sometimes we look for it there.How do we see the manifestations of vanity in our life? Looking for social position, worrying about the esteem of other people, even sometimes looking for positions within the Church.

And how does pride manifest itself? Self- sufficiency, an independent streak: "I don't need others," "I'll fend for myself," "I'll change myself."

Here's a quick test to see if you have made an idol of one of the 3 Ps in your life. Ask yourself three simple and similar questions and they will tell you if you are seeking your security in one of these three Ps. The first question we can ask ourselves: Do I lose peace when I see one of my things disappear or threatened?

There is a great story about St Lawrence (c. 225–258 AD) who was a deacon in the early church. He served under Pope Sixtus II during the time of the persecution of the Roman Emperor Valerian. After Valerian had captured and beheaded the Pope, Deacon Lawrence received a demand to gather the treasures of the Church to give over to the emperor. Lawrence requested three days to gather the treasures, then went out to the highways and byways of Rome to gather up all the treasures of the Catholic Church and bring them to the front of the door of the palace. The emperor opened the door and looked outside, expecting piles of money and gold and silver chalices, and all these things that he heard that the Catholic Church possessed. Instead he saw this crowd of ragamuffins, derelicts, cripples, and sick people. He asked Lawrence, "Where are the treasures of the Church?" and Lawrence answered, "Here we are, the treasures of the Church."

Needless to say, the emperor was not very amused, and Lawrence proceeded to get grilled, not with questions but with an actual grill. They stoked a fire, put him on the grill, and proceeded to roast him. Lawrence kept his wits about him, and after a few minutes called out to the soldiers to say, "I think I am done on this side; you can flip me over."

The second question we can ask ourselves to see where we place our security: Do I lose peace when I am misunderstood or overlooked? That's a tough one.

This reminds me of a story of St. Therese of Lisieux, who loved God so much that she asked to be just like a little toy in his hands. In her biography she wrote,

> *I had offered myself to the Child Jesus to be His little plaything. I told Him not to treat me like one of those precious toys which children only look at and dare not touch, but to treat me like a little ball of no value, that could be thrown on the ground, kicked about, pierced, left in a corner, or pressed to his Heart just as it might please him.*[21]

A third question we can ask ourselves: Do I lose peace in spiritual dryness, in spiritual deserts, or when I lose control of the situation? Fr. Walter Ciszek was an American priest who in his book He Leadeth Me relates the moment of his deepest conversion. As a strong-willed and idealistic young Jesuit, he had volunteered for a mission to the Soviet Union, but within days of his arrival there he was captured, interrogated as a purported Vatican spy, tortured, and left in solitary confinement in the notorious Lubyanka prison of Moscow. After months of firm resistance, he one day cracked. His human strength and resistance gave way, and he signed a false confession statement. The experience of his fragility and brokenness, though, became the start of a deeper spiritual life relying on God's will, not his own.

21   St. Therese of Lisieux, *Story of a Soul*, p. 91, Cosimo, New York, 2007.

Luc-Olivier Merson, Rest on the Flight into Egypt, 1879, Museum of Fine Arts, Boston, https://www.
mfa.org/collections/object/rest-on-the-flight-into-egypt-31734.

The past, with all its failures, was not forgotten; it
remained to remind me of the weakness of human
nature and the folly of putting any faith in self. But
it no longer depressed me. I looked no longer to self
to guide me, relied on it no longer in any way, so it
could not again fail me. By renouncing, finally and
completely, all control of my life and future destiny,
I was relieved as a consequence of all responsibility.
I was freed thereby from anxiety and worry, from
every tension, and could float serenely upon the tide of
God's sustaining providence in perfect peace of soul.[22]

If you lose peace in any of those three scenarios you may be building your
life on sand. The three Ps are sand. They wash away in the storms of life.
Where do you lose peace? Where is your treasure? Where is your heart?

Both men and women find their deepest security when they encounter
a God who loves them unconditionally, who calls them to follow him,

---

22   Fr. Walter Ciszek, SJ, He Leadeth Me.

and in doing so discover their life mission. This search manifests itself differently in each person, but ultimately, we all want to love and be loved. And love is the only foundation upon which we can build our lives.

> In the Church's Liturgy, in her prayer, in the living community of believers, we experience the love of God, we perceive his presence, and we thus learn to recognize that presence in our daily lives. He has loved us first and he continues to do so; we too, then, can respond with love. God does not demand of us a feeling which we ourselves are incapable of producing. He loves us, he makes us see and experience his love, and since he has "loved us first," love can also blossom as a response within us.[23]

Mary and Joseph were human, just as we are. They experienced the desire for security. They experienced danger and the adrenaline rush as they made their escape from Herod's sword. As we enter the second sorrow of Mary, the flight into Egypt, the human reality of our search for security can help us to understand more deeply her sorrow, as well as how she transformed it into joy.

---

23   Pope Benedict XVI, Deus Caritas Est, n. 17.

HOW DID THE FLIGHT INTO EGYPT PIERCE MARY'S HEART?

If all the food you ever ate was bland and unseasoned, you'd never miss salt and spices. If you'd never had indoor plumbing or a washing machine, you wouldn't think twice about using an outhouse or spending hours of your day cleaning clothes. When we lose something, that's when we begin to appreciate more fully just how good we had it.

This simple truth helps us to understand why the flight into Egypt was such a deep sorrow for Mary. Put yourself in her shoes for a moment. Her life had been one of many simple joys. For the past months, she has experienced the solicitude of Joseph, attentive to her every need; the visit of shepherds who speak of marvelous visitations from angelic hosts; the kingly gifts of wise men who have traveled hundreds of miles "to do him homage" (Mt 2:2). Mary is esteemed and blessed. Sure, there have been some privations, but all in all, life has been good. Simeon's prophecy and the doting presence of Anna in the Temple has brought attention to Mary and her child, inviting the esteem of those around her and bubbling excitement among the passersby in the Temple. The worry she feels at his words is outweighed by the exhilaration that rose in her bosom upon hearing the prophecy and the expectation that something great was about to happen. Yes, sometimes it does feel good to be in the spotlight, to be loved, to be noticed.

But one man changes all that. Herod. That despotic ruler who is so possessive of his power that he killed his own sons to keep them from usurping the throne. Herod gets wind of a new threat to his power.

> *Magi from the east arrived in Jerusalem, saying,*
> *"Where is the newborn king of the Jews? We saw his*
> *star at its rising and have come to do him homage."*
> *When King Herod heard this, he was greatly troubled,*
> *and all Jerusalem with him.*
> *Matthew 2:1–3*

All Jerusalem is troubled, because when Herod is insecure, no one else's life is secure. We all know people like that. Perhaps we are like that. Personal insecurity breeds instability, lack of peace, lashing out. It's like someone who is drowning and flails about wildly in the water, even pushing underwater those who come to the rescue. In a desperate effort to stay above water, the insecure person will bring down everyone else. Insecurity. Herod feels the water rising. So those around him get nervous.

> *Assembling all the chief priests and the scribes of the*
> *people, he inquired of them where the Messiah was to*
> *be born. They said to him, "In Bethlehem of Judea,*
> *for thus it has been written through the prophet: 'And*
> *you, Bethlehem, land of Judah, are by no means least*
> *among the rulers of Judah; since from you shall come a*
> *ruler, who is to shepherd my people Israel."*
> Matthew 2:4–6

What is remarkable about this statement from the chief priests and scribes isn't what they say, but what they don't do. They clearly know the Scriptures and prophecy. They know, but they do not act. They remain in Jerusalem. They do not run to Bethlehem as did the shepherds. They do not seek out their own Messiah, even when they witness foreign rulers who come to pay homage to their newborn king. Why? Not from ignorance, but from lethargy. They are comfortable in their ways. They've put their security in wealth, worldly honor, and the status quo. They are afraid of Herod and don't want to upset the delicate balance in their comfortable lives. Not only do they miss the moment, but they also miss the One who alone could give them true security.

But while the religious leaders are complacent, Herod is on the move.

> *Then Herod called the magi secretly and ascertained*
> *from them the time of the star's appearance. He sent*
> *them to Bethlehem and said, "Go and search diligently*
> *for the child. When you have found him, bring me*
> *word, that I too may go and do him homage."*
> Matthew 2:7–8

What a liar! Deception, manipulation, dark deeds. All these are spawned when someone seeks security in the wrong places. Herod has no intention of worshiping the Messiah. He wants this threat to his power eliminated, and he will stop at nothing until it is gone.

Meanwhile, the magi make it to the manger.

> *"And on entering the house they saw the child with*
> *Mary his mother. They prostrated themselves and did*
> *him homage. Then they opened their treasures and*
> *offered him gifts of gold, frankincense, and myrrh."*
> Matthew 2:11

Mary's heart must have raced with exhilaration at this visit from the magi. She could see the prophecies being fulfilled. Her son is being recognized as the long-awaited Messiah, the true King of Kings. Yes, he *would* bring about the rise and fall of many in Israel. Perhaps now is the time to depose that tyrant, Herod! And these gifts! Regal gifts of gold, frankincense, and myrrh. God has provided for all their needs and more.

And yet just when the future appears the brightest, the darkness of sorrow descends.

> *When they had departed, behold, the angel of the Lord*
> *appeared to Joseph in a dream and said, 'Rise, take*
> *the child and his mother, flee to Egypt, and stay there*
> *until I tell you. Herod is going to search for the child*
> *to destroy him.' Joseph rose and took the child and his*
> *mother by night and departed for Egypt.*
> Matthew 2:13–14

No! No! No! Everything is wrong with this picture. If God wanted to show his power, this is the moment to manifest it! The Messiah is born; foreign powers are present as witnesses; depose the dictator and re-establish the Davidic dynasty! Things are on a roll!

But God's ways are not man's ways.

The song written by one of the Consecrated Women of Regnum Christi called "Through the Desert" was referenced at the beginning of this chapter. Listen again to it now and try understand a little bit more of what Mary was going through at this moment in her life, as she had to take up all her possessions and flee into Egypt. We all experience deserts in our life. We all experience difficult moments when things are not so clear and when we struggle.

God's ways are not man's ways. Security does not come from the power of this world, nor from its esteem and comforts. Instead of power,

God chooses persecution. Flight, not fight. His divine Son becomes a refugee, an outcast, an immigrant. Joseph and Mary leave behind the security of their homeland to cast out into the unknown. And think of her situation: Mary has only been with Joseph for a few months, is still getting to know him, and now it is just the two of them with a baby. They have no chance to say goodbye to friends or family, to let them know where they are going, to give a forwarding address.

They brave the physical privations of a long journey through desert wastelands. They face the emotional privations of being separated from all that is familiar and loved. They are immigrants. They enter a country with a new language that they do not speak, with different traditions, distinct religious practices, and cultural expectations that they just don't understand. In some sense they are political refugees, fleeing Israel with the constant fear of being discovered, of having Herod's thugs track them down and finish the job.

If you've never lived in another country where you do not speak the language, you cannot fully understand the great angst and insecurity it creates. You feel stupid, useless, always an outsider. You can never express yourself fully, even when you've learned the rudiments of the language. You are the butt of many jokes and sly looks of mutual understanding between others. You are mentally drained by the effort to listen, to understand, to speak. Everything must be re-learned. And when you encounter someone who does speak your language, or a fellow countryman, an indescribable joy wells up within your soul and you begin to speak with bubbly excitement in your native tongue. Finally, someone who can understand you!

In this situation that Mary and Joseph faced, the native-born sons of Egypt look down on the new arrivals. They are mistreated. They are labeled by those around them and discriminated against for wearing different clothes, speaking with an accent. They hear the barely disguised hostility as passersby talk about "those immigrants who steal our jobs" or about the "leeches on our great country." Their first accommodations are shabby, and Joseph's search for work and a livelihood tak time to materialize. He gets cheated and taken advantage of. In the meantime, they experience more poverty and empty stomachs for Joseph and Mary. So many unknowns, so little security. Other Jewish emigres perhaps provided some solace, but did not alleviate all their suffering.

Amid these circumstances, Mary must at least contemplate the possibility that her son will grow up without family connections, and no tie to his cultural heritage. And as the months pass by, the unknowns do not diminish.

On top of all these causes for insecurity comes one that touches her sensitive spirit in a particularly deep way. She has had no dream. The angel is now speaking to Joseph, not to her. She's left in the dark. God is not guiding Mary directly, but asking her to trust her husband. Joseph is now the one receiving the divine commands, and there is at least a temptation to wonder if she's done something wrong or to question why she's being excluded from the direct communication. It is a direct challenge to pride when we must acknowledge and follow the lead of someone else, even when that someone else is a dearly loved husband. Yet there is also joy in following those who are listening to and leading us to God.

All of this and more, more than we will ever know in this life, Mary and Joseph experience in Egypt. She has lost all that is familiar and secure. Mary's sorrow is real. It is deep.

MARY'S SORROW TRANSFORMED INTO JOY

So how did Mary transform the sorrow of the flight to Egypt into joy?

As a daughter of Israel, Mary would have memorized many of the Psalms, particularly Psalm 23. Now the words would come back to her during those long lonely nights crossing the desert, fleeing from a ruthless ruler.

> *The LORD is my shepherd; there is nothing I lack.*
> *In green pastures you let me graze; to safe waters you*
> *lead me; you restore my strength. You guide me along*
> *the right path for the sake of your name. Even when I*
> *walk through a dark valley, I fear no harm for you are*
> *at my side; your rod and staff give me courage. You set*
> *a table before me as my enemies watch; You anoint my*
> *head with oil; my cup overflows. Only goodness and*
> *love will pursue me all the days of my life; I will dwell*
> *in the house of the LORD for years to come.*
> *Psalm 23:1–6*

As we reflect on these words from scripture, just as Mary did as she crossed that desert and entered this new land, listen to the song "I Shall Not Want" by Audrey Assad.[24]

The Blessed Virgin Mary is indeed a daughter of Israel. As she experiences the sorrow of flight, her heart and mind may be retracing the steps of Abraham, Isaac, Jacob, Joseph, and Moses through the desert. She may recall King David, the great psalmist, during his years of exile in the wilderness. Like him, she could have prayed:

> *Some wandered in desert wastelands, finding no way to a city where they could settle. They were hungry and thirsty, and their lives ebbed away. Then they cried out to the Lord in their trouble, and he delivered them from their distress. He led them by a straight way to a city where they could settle. Let them give thanks to the Lord for his unfailing love and his wonderful deeds for mankind, for he satisfies the thirsty and fills the hungry with good things.*
> *Psalm 107: 4–9*

As we contemplate how she faces this suffering of exile into Egypt, we can begin to understand three simple steps she took to transform sorrow into joy.

1. She builds upon her experience after Simeon's prophecy. There, she had learned not to succumb to worry. She grows in her trust by recognizing God's hand in the past, living the present in his love, and acknowledging his provident power over the future.

2. God leads her through a real desert and a spiritual one. She lets go of all human security, whether in creature comforts, the esteem of others, or her own self-sufficiency. She is not merely forced to do this; Mary embraces and chooses to relinquish those things that could never really provide security anyway, thus growing in the virtues that lead to security:

   ◇ *Temperance.* Mary lets go of the simple comforts because she would not let anything come between

---

her and Jesus. She will embrace any privation out of love for him.

◇ *Simplicity.* Mary bases her worth not on the opinion of others (vanity), and not on the lack of esteem that people heap upon her as she comes as an immigrant into a foreign land. She bases her worth, her dignity, on God's love for her, on her God-given dignity.

◇ *Humility.* Mary grows in the virtue of humility. She shows it in trusting Joseph and following his lead, and trusting in God's plan and Providence in the midst of this dark valley.

3. The Virgin Mary grasps onto her Lord more firmly, placing her security in God alone. He is her rock, her fortress. As St. Teresa of Avila stated so well, "Let nothing trouble you. Let nothing frighten you. Everything passes. God never changes. Patience obtains all. Whoever has God wants for nothing. God alone is enough."

Because Mary did this throughout her exile, she lived out what St. Paul would later write in his letter to the Philippians.

Rejoice in the Lord always. I shall say it again: rejoice! Your kindness should be known to all. The Lord is near. Have no anxiety at all, but in everything, by prayer and petition, with thanksgiving, make your requests known to God. Then the peace of God that surpasses all understanding will guard your hearts and minds in Christ Jesus.
Philippians 4:4–7

The Virgin Mary's joys are profound, not because she didn't have problems and obstacles in her life, but because her heart came through the desert into deepened relationships with Jesus and Joseph (shared sufferings forge the deepest bonds), into new relationships and new experiences in Egypt, and into a deeper trust in God's Providence. Gazing upon her son gave her consolation and confidence. In her Lord, she found the only security that is unshakeable, and could live in "the peace of God that surpasses all understanding."

Peace is a fruit of the Holy Spirit's presence in our life. Throughout the flight into Egypt, the Holy Spirit gave Mary his gift of understanding in a deeper way, allowing her to *read into*—"*intus legere*" in Latin, where we get the word "intelligence"—the inner workings of the heart. Understanding counters dullness of heart and allows us to move beyond a life built on the sand of human securities. Like Mary, may we come through the deserts of our life understanding the instability of sand, emptying it from our shoes, and seeking the security of him who alone is rock and refuge.

> *Be my rock and refuge, my secure stronghold; for*
> *you are my rock and fortress. My God, rescue me*
> *from the power of the wicked, from the clutches of*
> *the violent. You are my hope, Lord; my trust, GOD,*
> *from my youth.*
> Psalm 71:3–5

QUESTIONS FOR PERSONAL REFLECTION OR DISCUSSION

1. Am I still insecure in some ways? Where do I find my security?

2. What are some ways that I still seek creature comforts, the accolades and esteem of others, or control of everything myself? How do I grow in my trust, and in what areas do I need to place my security in God?

3. Do I have compassion on those who are rejected, unwanted, or on the fringes of society? Where do I encounter these people in my life? How do I treat them? Am I so insecure that I am afraid to associate with them in any way, lest my own reputation be brought down?

4. Like the Blessed Virgin Mary, do I find strength and peace through belief in God's loving presence, even amid turmoil and daunting obstacles?

5. How am I growing in understanding, the gift of the Holy Spirit that helps me to see into the deeper reality of things, relate all truths to my supernatural purpose, and appreciate God's loving Providence in all that happens?

6. How does that understanding help me to put my security in the Lord, rather than in things, others, or self? Have I asked for this gift in my prayer?

AN INVITATION TO PRAYER

Virgin of Nazareth, Mother in Bethlehem, your struggles and sorrows grow as you become a refugee in Egypt, an immigrant in a foreign land. Mary, your trust in the Lord did not remove all the obstacles in your life, but by believing and trusting that he gave you grace to overcome them all. You found inner peace in the midst of the turmoil all around. Blessed Virgin Mary, you, too, were tempted to put your security in familiar comforts, in the esteem of those around you, or in your own understanding and abilities ... but you had the wisdom to seek security in the Lord alone. Help me to humble my pride, to laugh away my vanity, and to embrace privations so that I, too, can trust in the Lord alone. He is my rock, my fortress, my deliverer. Mother, teach me to trust. Mother, teach me to reach out compassionately to the outcasts on the fringes of society, the refugees and immigrants, the unwanted, the lost. All of them are beloved in the eyes of God. Teach me to see them and to love them as he does.

Hail Mary full of grace ...

Jesus, I trust in you!

CHAPTER 3

THE LOSS OF JESUS IN THE TEMPLE

"Lo, I am sending my messenger to prepare the way before me; And suddenly there will come to the temple the LORD whom you seek, And the messenger of the covenant whom you desire. Yes, he is coming, says the LORD of hosts."
Malachi 3:1

Steve Dunwell, Mary and Jesus, stained glass, Our Lady of Victories Church (now closed), Bay Village, Boston, Massachusetts, USA. https://www.agefotostock.com/age/en/Stock-Images/Rights-Managed/J10-2632323

William Holman Hunt, The Finding of the Saviour in the Temple, 1860, Birmingham Museum and Art Gallery, https://en.wikipedia.org/wiki/The_Finding_of_the_Saviour_in_the_Temple#/media/ File:William_Holman_Hunt_-_The_Finding_of_the_Saviour_in_the_Temple.jpg.

SACRED MUSIC TO AID CONTEMPLATION

◇ *Te Joseph Celebrent* by Benedictines of Mary[25]

◇ *Here with Us* by Joy Williams[26]

HOLINESS IN THE HUMDRUM

In the first chapters, we've entered the heart of the Blessed Virgin Mary, getting to know her sorrows and joys intimately, experientially. She's become a closer companion in our own life. We've seen how love makes us vulnerable to sorrow, but it's also the secret to the deepest happiness. Mary suffered, yet no human person before or since has also experienced the depth of joy and fulfillment that she did. In her womb grew the Son of God; at her breasts fed the Savior of the World; on her knees she taught the One who receives our prayers how to pray;

---

25   https://www.youtube.com/watch?v=LFTldyRNA7E
26   https://www.youtube.com/watch?v=EosUH0orVUg

at her table sat the Bread of Life. After the danger of Herod's jealous fury had passed, Jesus, Mary, and Joseph resettled in the quiet hamlet of Nazareth. Those years of Jesus' childhood—despite the haunting prophecy of Simeon and the exile in Egypt—were filled with the most intimate moments of love and joy. Life is good. The simple daily chores—stoking the cooking fire, carrying jars of water from the well, bathing Jesus, baking bread—are carried out in love. Joseph brings Mary wildflowers from the meadow and never forgets to thank her for all she does each day while he's at work. Mary discovers his tastes so she can prepare his favorite meals, and always finds a way to praise him behind his back with her friends, proud of what a faithful husband and protector God has provided her and Jesus. And the little child Jesus is growing, talking, and running around with the neighborhood kids, just like all the other children.

Yet in this idyllic world, sinister clouds begin to gather again on the horizon of her heart. Temptations to doubt, to impatience, to dissatisfaction with her lot in life. What was happening with the angel's prophecy? Jesus wasn't doing anything special. Wasn't he supposed to save his people? He hadn't been called up to the Sanhedrin—the inner power circle of elders of the Jewish people—or to Herod's court. Roman rulers continue to control their land. And she is tempted to fear. What is coming? Is she a good mother? Is she doing everything she could to help him? Will she know how to form and guide her son to carry out his mission? What more is she supposed to do?

And through all this, silence. No revelations. No dreams. No angels. No prophets to arrive and make things clear. So, Mary simply prays and follows the religious practices handed down to her. She continued to walk in faith, without seeing everything clearly.

Our lives are no different. Occasionally we have a mountaintop experience: we see God's plan clearly, experience his tremendous love, get emotional and exhilarated and hyper-focused on what must be done—and then we descend into the dark valley of everyday humdrum existence. Maybe it's your boring, dead-end job. Perhaps it's the never-ending cycle of mindless laundry, cooking, and chores inherent in running a household. For others it's the same questions and self-doubt about raising a child that Mary experienced ... or perhaps concern for a child who has gone astray. For all of us, we experience the dark clouds, the obscurity, the indecision, the questioning whether I'm doing the right thing, or if I'm doing enough, or if I might just be the biggest failure ever.

We want clarity, excitement … but instead there seems to be only drudgery, putting one foot in front of the other.

It is precisely here that the Virgin Mary's third sorrow can provide us profound insights into life, so we can see how to face our failures in faith, and grow in the happiness and holiness God wants for us. Let's dig a bit deeper now into the loss of Jesus in the Temple.

HOW DID THE LOSS OF JESUS IN THE TEMPLE PIERCE MARY'S HEART?

Let's first put ourselves into the scene, drawing out in a contemplative manner what could have transpired. In each chapter, these contemplative speculations are neither private revelation nor statements of fact, but rather poetic license musing about how things might have been, and what the Virgin Mary could possibly have felt or said or done. Hopefully, you will find the reflections helpful and a launching point for your own prayer.

In Luke 2:41 we read: "Each year his parents went to Jerusalem for the feast of Passover, and when he was twelve years old, they went up according to festival custom."

"Each year." Mary and Joseph completed all the religious duties of a pious Jew, never neglecting the Law despite the inconveniences this must have caused. Several days of travel exposed to the heat, cold, or rain; the discomfort of sleeping on the ground surrounded by strangers; the extra cost and disruption of a regular work and home routine. And we complain about driving to Mass for an hour on Sunday! Not all the Jews went to Jerusalem each year, but Mary and Joseph did. They didn't find excuses for themselves, despite having a small child, a business to run, and plenty of friends and neighbors who were too busy to go worship God.

Each year they went up to Jerusalem, that hub of the Jewish people. There was the Temple, focal point for their worship of God. According to some accounts, Mary herself had lived there in the Temple as a little girl, and she must have felt such joy returning to those old familiar stone walls, archways, sounds of bleating lambs and market cries, the smells of massed humanity mixed with incense and burnt offerings. Ah, Jerusalem! Home of the patriarchs of faith, sepulcher for the prophets. A city of sinners and saints. A city that Jesus, too, was finding more and more familiar with as the years passed, and by 12 years old he feels right at home there.

A few years ago, while in Jerusalem for a pilgrimage, I was able to witness firsthand the *bar mitzvah* ceremony of a Jewish boy. We were waiting in a long line to pass through security into the area near the

Georges de La Tour, Joseph the Carpenter 1645 Louvre, Paris. https://en.wikipedia.org/wiki/Joseph_the_Carpenter#/media/File:La_Tour.jpg

Wailing Wall, the last remnants of the Temple of Herod that Jesus himself visited as a boy. While we waited for hours in the hot sun, no one complained. There was a festive air. On that sabbath day, dozens of groups clustered around distinct 12-year-old boys who were coming to celebrate their passage to manhood. Traditional instruments—long curved ram's horns, tambourines, pipes, and small drums—filled the air with joyful tunes while both men and women danced circles around their boys. It was an open-air party, and everyone laughed and delighted and wished each other well in multiple languages. That day we were all Jewish—and we loved it.

Jesus celebrated something similar that year. Mary was so proud of him! Her son was becoming a man. Joseph must have grasped his shoulders, looked firmly down into his eyes, and congratulated him. Jesus' own heart must have filled with a sense of importance, of maturity, of mission. He is now an adult member of the community. He can now speak in the synagogue, join the men in prayer, and leave behind the outer court of the Temple.

Into this celebratory scene crash the words of Scripture:

> "After they had completed its days, as they were
> returning, the boy Jesus remained behind in Jerusalem,
> but his parents did not know it. Thinking that he was in
> the caravan, they journeyed for a day and looked for him
> among their relatives and acquaintances, but not finding
> him, they returned to Jerusalem to look for him."
> Luke 2:43–45

Every mother has a protective, nurturing instinct. Harm her child, and you'll have an enemy forever. Should she harm her own child, only with the greatest of grace will she ever forgive herself. That is why the pain of losing a child—no matter how it happens—is so hard for a woman. A few years ago, I spoke with a woman who had accidentally backed her Suburban over her 2-year-old child; sorrow that deep finds no easy consolation. On dozens of occasions I've heard confessions of women who aborted their child. No matter how well she may have justified it at the time, the truth of what she did to her own innocent child will not be forgotten and it haunts her even decades later; but even that sin is not too great for God's mercy, and I've seen the healing that God brings through the sacrament of confession.

Every mother was made to nourish, nurture, and instruct her children. In this calling, there also seems to be an innate fear that she might fail as a mother, let her children down, or not do everything possible for them to succeed.

And this fear of failure clamps at Mary's throat now. "Where is Jesus?" She'd seen him during the procession to the Temple, and then he'd been with Joseph and the men for the celebrations. She'd gone to make merry with her girlfriends, trusting that Joseph would keep an eye on Jesus. And they'd begun the return journey to Galilee with the caravan just like they usually did, the men walking together and swapping stories and joking, while the children and women walked or rode together and caught each other up on the latest news and chatted excitedly about the celebrations of the past days. Mary knew Jesus was with the men now, so she didn't think twice about not seeing Jesus with her and the little boys and girls in the caravan; Joseph hadn't noticed anything at all. That night when they met to set up their tent for the night, Mary must have looked at Joseph quizzically, with a mounting sense of fear as she asks, "Where is Jesus?" And Joseph sounds neither confident nor intelligent as he looks up in surprise and questions, "Wasn't he with you?"

Mary says nothing. No condemning words, no harsh remarks, no nagging Joseph for his negligence. If that's not the greatest proof of her holiness right there! How quick we are to blame others, to get annoyed with our husband, to belittle him! Mary says nothing. Immediately, they both understand the situation. Joseph doesn't need Mary to highlight his mistake. He's a smart man. Their love and concern are immediate, and together they set out to find Jesus among their relatives and acquaintances in the caravan. He can't be too far away. They aren't too worried yet, and Mary holds in check the temptation to fear in her heart.

Joseph circles one way through the caravan, Mary the other. Minutes later they return, each searching the eyes of the other, as worry mounts. "Mary, anything?" "No, Joseph." They recount the day's travel and quickly realize that Jesus must still be in Jerusalem. Thankfully, they are still a short distance away, though they must wait out the night, when searching would be useless. As Mary attempts to sleep that night, her mind must be racing with every possible outcome—and the recriminating thoughts: "How could I have left Jesus behind? What kind of a mother am I? I'm a failure!"

Before the crack of dawn, with tired and bloodshot eyes, Mary and Joseph began sweeping the familiar streets of Jerusalem. Nothing. Every hour that passes by without finding Jesus augments their anxiety. All day they search, asking street vendors, looking through the markets, questioning each passerby who would listen, "Have you seen a boy? His name is Jesus, and he's 12 and about this tall, and…." Everyone had seen boys. Hundreds of them, many matching the description. One lead after another turns out to be a wild goose chase, and with each failed attempt, Mary's fears surge. Voices in her head scream out, "Failure! You are a failure as a mother! You cannot even keep your son safe!" And how could she see it otherwise? She couldn't bring herself to accuse Joseph. It was all her fault. "If I'd been a little more attentive … if I'd have asked sooner … if I had reminded Joseph … if, if, if …"

Her mind runs wild with doomsday scenarios. After all she had done to protect Jesus from Herod, perhaps his successors had found him. Herod might be dead, but there were plenty of other rapacious rulers and ruffians about to kill, kidnap for ransom, or sell unattached children into slavery or the pleasure trade. Mary's mind plays out all these scenes with horror as the twilight and then darkness set in. A day of searching done. Nothing to show for it. Joseph and Mary ask about for a few more fruitless hours, then huddle together in the shelter of an archway while troubled dreams disrupt their few hours of fitful sleep.

Morning breaks long after they've renewed the hunt for Jesus. Empty stomachs, not fed for nearly two days now, growl and are ignored. They are hungry for something more important than food right now. Mary and Joseph peer into dark corners, question shady characters, and expand their search to the foulest quarters of the city. Nothing. A few people show concern for their plight, but no one joins them to find Jesus, and indifference toward their loss is the most common reaction. And all the while the voices inside call out what a failure she is. "Useless! How could you lose the Son of God? Do you realize what horrific punishment will be in store for you? What a failure!"

In this darkest moment of desperation, Mary recalls her roots. She turns to God in prayer. Once again, the words of Psalm 23 ring out in her mind: "Even when I walk through a dark valley, I fear no harm for you are at my side; your rod and staff give me courage … I will dwell in the house of the LORD for years to come." Yes, prayer calms her spirit. Prayer is not merely a psychological ploy, a self-help technique to deal with stress and guilt. No, prayer is much more. It's more because there's Someone besides myself behind it. "You" are at my side. The Lord is the one who inspires trust and removes the fear. What child worries when

William Holman Hunt, The Finding of the Saviour in the Temple, 1860, Birmingham Museum and
Art Gallery, https://en.wikipedia.org/wiki/The_Finding_of_the_Saviour_in_the_Temple#/media/
File:William_Holman_Hunt_-_The_Finding_of_the_Saviour_in_the_Temple.jpg.

held in the strong arms of their father? How can we fear if we truly
believe that he cares for us? Prayer calms Mary's spirit, and then brings
her mind back to the promise: "I will dwell in the house of the Lord."
Prayer sparks insights. "Joseph, the Temple! We haven't yet looked in
the house of the Lord!"

And, as is usually the case in our own lives, once they had exhausted
their own feeble efforts and turned to God's power in prayer, the desired
results come. There he is! As Luke relates:

> *After three days they found him in the temple, sitting*
> *in the midst of the teachers, listening to them and*
> *asking them questions, and all who heard him were*
> *astounded at his understanding and his answers.*
> *Luke 2:46*

From Jesus's perspective, it must have been very simple. He was now
an adult, so he saw no problem in sticking around where he felt at
home... in the Temple of God the Almighty, and beginning to engage
in his mission. He listened. He asked insightful questions. He excited

admiration in all who heard him. Luke continues:

> *When his parents saw him, they were astonished, and*
> *his mother said to him, 'Son, why have you done this*
> *to us? Your father and I have been looking for you*
> *with great anxiety.'*
> *Luke 2:48*

What an understatement!

And upon seeing them, does Jesus leap up in joy and cry out, "My mother, how I missed you. I've been completely distraught looking for you everywhere. I will never leave your side again, as long as I live!"?

Probably not. On the contrary, we have the cryptic words that Luke relates:

> *And he said to them, "Why were you looking for me? Did*
> *you not know that I must be in my Father's house?"But*
> *they did not understand what he said to them.*
> *Luke 2:49*

Mary did not understand his words, and only with the 20/20 vision that hindsight gives are we able to understand. Jesus does not reciprocate Mary's joy and relief. Instead, he seems to dismiss her worries in a cavalier, almost flippant, manner. "Why were you looking for me?" What mother would not look for her lost child? Because she loved him, she had searched so frantically for him. Could he not see that? Did he not perceive her concern?

Yes, Jesus does recognize her sorrow, but he is already trying to move her heart to the deeper joy and her deeper calling. Mary was overwhelmed by the loss; Jesus wants her to move forward with him to what is gained: the Father's house.

In the life of every mother and son, there comes a moment of emotional separation. When he's a little boy, he's so affectionate and close to mom. But a time comes when the boundaries shift, when he takes a step toward manhood, when he pushes away the hugs and doesn't want to be seen with "Mommy," when he chooses his father or his friends over her. He chooses to be with others instead of her, and she almost feels as if she's lost a popularity contest; that's never easy for any woman.

In the case of Mary and Jesus, this separation is also the harbinger of things to come, a prelude to further separation, sorrow, the Passion and the Cross. What was prophesied by Simeon is not over by any means, but is just beginning, and Mary feels the sword pierce her heart. Jesus has taken a first step on the path toward the Father's house. Every mother who has a child take a step toward a life of total consecration to Jesus—as a priest, brother, sister, or consecrated person—feels what Mary felt: the sorrow of loss and separation, yet also the joy of something new on the horizon.

If we lose Jesus, all is lost. Mary felt that loss deeply during those three desperate days. But when we find him, when we return to him—*con-vertere*, to turn back, to convert—through prayer and the sacrament of reconciliation, we gain more than we had ever lost. This is the experience of every Christian. We are not perfect. We don't have it all together. We are not a bunch of self-righteous prigs who've never done anything wrong in our lives; we are sinners who have experienced the forgiveness and mercy of God the Father time and time again, and through that unconditional love have come to realize that the best place to be is "in my Father's house." Jesus knew this. He reminded his mother of this. He wants to lead you and me to this: to be in the Father's house.

And so, Luke finishes the narrative with these encouraging words:

> *He went down with them and came to Nazareth, and*
> *was obedient to them; and his mother kept all these*
> *things in her heart. And Jesus advanced (in) wisdom*
> *and age and favor before God and man.*
> Luke 2:51

Mary had much to ponder. So do we. Looking into Mary's heart and mind through the loss of Jesus in the Temple, we can see in her sorrow three lessons:

1. In her own interior, Mary wrestles with her self-doubt, the negativity, the wild imagination, the fear of failure. But she does not let that rule her or shut her down. She lives the words that John would later write in his epistle, perhaps because she

herself taught him this in the years after Jesus's death when
John cared for her in Ephesus as his own mother. John wrote:
"There is no fear in love, but perfect love drives out fear." (1
John 4:18) Through this terrible experience of loss, Mary grows
in love, and that love drives away all fear. This is the secret for
us to overcome fear: Love! And love is more than a feeling; it
is commitment and self-giving to bring about the good of the
other.

2. Mary doesn't let sorrow drive a wedge between herself and
   Joseph. We are so quick to blame others, to find someone
   to pin the fault on besides ourselves. Mary resists that urge.
   She doesn't chide or nag her husband, and Joseph isn't
   condescending or critical of his wife. She doesn't rub his
   failures into his face. She doesn't urge Joseph to discipline
   Jesus for his cheeky response to their concern and anxiety. She
   trusts, loves, supports, builds upon the positive, and does not
   place unrealistic expectations upon the man who has received a
   mission that surpasses his human capacity. They both put their
   ultimate trust in God, and support each other as best they can.

3. Mary began to learn how to relate to Jesus in a new way. She
   needed to learn how to let go, just as every mother must learn
   to allow their children space to fall, to spread their wings, and
   to take their own path in life. From the spiritual perspective,
   perhaps in our first years of life we had deep experiences of
   Jesus. Maybe we later passed through a stage of your life where
   we rebelled not only against our parents, but also against
   God and his plan for our happiness, wandering the lonely and
   barren wastelands of self-determination and sin. Though Mary
   never sinned, she did have to learn to relate to Jesus in a new
   way, with different parameters. We are each called to leave
   behind our sinfulness and rebelliousness, and to see in Jesus
   more than a historical figure or a pious childhood story. He is
   real. He is love. He loves us. He has a mission that he calls us to
   participate in: to bring all people to the Father's house. That is
   where we will find our ultimate fulfillment.

MARY'S SORROW TRANSFORMED INTO JOY

The Blessed Virgin Mary's experience of sorrow at the loss of Jesus in the Temple and during the long hours of fruitless searching leads her to greater depth in her interior life. Her sorrow becomes joy as she looks beyond the present suffering. "His mother kept all these things in her heart" (Luke 2:52). She prays, she meditates, so she doesn't grow embittered but, as a good mother, sees things more from the Father's perspective. This is the fruit of prayer, shown in three ways.

1. The first thing she may have received in her prayer is perspective on Jesus' vocational choice: what a noble path her son has taken! He's not with a gang of hooligans; he's not using other people; he's not making destructive life choices or just thinking about his own career path and happiness. He's with the chief priests in the Temple; he is seeking God the Father's plan. Occasionally I have met moms who are afraid that their son or daughter might be called to the priesthood or consecrated life. Perhaps they don't understand this vocation to total love; perhaps they don't realize that in all surveys, it is the life vocation with the highest degree of personal satisfaction, and that the renunciations also lead to deeper rewards, just as sorrow can lead to the deepest joys. Oh, if we understood the dignity of a vocation to the priesthood, we'd all pray so much more ardently for our child or grandchild to be called! Let us pray to the Lord of the harvest for many good and holy priests and consecrated souls! Let us pray to our Lord "lost" in the Temple that many more young men and women will lose themselves in his all-embracing love!

2. Joy comes from good that is possessed, and now more than ever, Mary feels a closeness to her son who returns with her to Nazareth. She hasn't lost her son after all. His momentary separation helps her to value more deeply their unique relationship. When we have Jesus, we have every good thing and the deepest of joy. That is enough for the present moment: to bask in the Son's love. Mary knows not what the future will bring, and we almost feel like crying out to her, "Get ready, Mary! This is just the beginning. Deeper separation and sorrow is coming!" But God only gives us as much as we can handle in each moment of our

lives, and if we trust in him, he will never give us more than we
can handle, we will never be broken, we will never fail.

3. Mary's sorrow is transformed into joy through her meditation
    on the beginning of Jesus's mission. The words of the prophets
    are coming true. Jesus—whose name means 'God saves'—is
    beginning to show his true colors, and she feels in her own soul
    a profound delight in the imminent redemption of her people.
    Joy comes not only from good that we possess, but even more
    so from good that we share. This is the joy of following our
    calling, from sharing the Good News.

We too ask for the grace to apprehend the truth in our lives, to see
everything from the Father's perspective, and to ponder all these things
in our hearts with the Holy Spirit's gift of counsel that guides fortitude
and protects against rashness.

QUESTIONS FOR PERSONAL REFLECTION OR DISCUSSION

1. What fears have been affecting my life recently? In what way
    have they dominated me, stolen my peace?

2. How could I experience the freedom and peace God desires for
    me, reflected in these words: "perfect love drives out fear" (1
    John 4:18)?

3. What was it that kept the Blessed Virgin Mary from blaming
    Joseph? What needs to change in my own heart, mind, or
    behavior so that I stop tearing others down with my words and
    instead build up and encourage those around me? Have I asked
    for God's grace in prayer, through the intercession of Mary, for
    these changes or do I think I can do it by myself?

4. How have I experienced separation from Jesus in my own life?
    Have I come now to a deeper relationship with him? What has
    helped me the most to strengthen my relationship with Christ?

5. What have the sources of joy been so far in my life? Have I
    experienced something of the deepest joys that come from the
    greatest good, God himself?

6. Have I experienced the joy of giving and sharing my own experience of God's goodness? Would I feel sorrow or joy if one of my children had a calling to the priesthood or consecrated life? Why? What would the Blessed Virgin Mary have to say to me about that?

AN INVITATION TO PRAYER

Blessed Virgin Mary, you experienced fear of failure so deeply at the loss of Jesus in the Temple, but you didn't let fear rule your heart, because "perfect love casts out all fear." Teach me to love Jesus more, to place my trust in him. Quiet the voices of negativity and guilt in my mind by a sincere conversion of my heart, through deeper confidence in Divine Mercy, and by availing myself of the Father's forgiveness through regular confession. Mary, help me to find Jesus in prayer, Scripture, the Eucharist, and the least of my brethren. When I see the hurt and pain in the lives of those who are lost, let me be your heart and hands and feet to reach out through the corporal and spiritual works of mercy to bring them home, to the Father's house. May I love with your Immaculate Heart, and with the Sacred Heart of your divine Son. Amen.

Hail Mary full of grace …

Jesus, I trust in you!

CHAPTER 4

MARY MEETS JESUS ON THE WAY TO CALVARY

"Whoever wishes to come after me must deny himself, take up his cross, and follow me. For whoever wishes to save his life will lose it, but whoever loses his life for my sake will find it."
Matthew 16:24–25

Hans Holbein, Mary as the Mother of Sorrows, 1495, Gemäldegalerie, Berlin.

SACRED MUSIC TO AID CONTEMPLATION

◇ *Making All Things New* by the Consecrated Women of
Regnum Christi[27]

LOSE IT TO FIND IT

Throughout our prayerful pondering of the first three sorrows of the
Blessed Virgin Mary, we've peered into and grown closer to her heart.
We've felt her fear, angst, and temptations to doubt, but more important
we've learned from her to overcome each temptation through faith and
deeper trust in God, widening our limited perspective to see things as
God does. He is a loving Father, and will never let us be tested beyond
what he gives us the grace to handle. And Mary is a loving mother,

> *Able to turn a stable into a home for Jesus, with poor
> swaddling clothes and an abundance of love. She is
> the handmaid of the Father who sings his praises. She
> is the friend who is ever concerned that wine not be
> lacking in our lives. She is the woman whose heart
> was pierced by a sword and who understands all our
> pain... As a true mother, she walks at our side, she
> shares our struggles, and she constantly surrounds us
> with God's love.*[28]

Mary is a true mother. She understands all our pain because she has
experienced it first. She helps us to transition from sorrow to joy,
because she has accomplished that first. And because she ponders all
these things in her heart, what happens to her son, even on the Way of
the Cross, does not steal her peace.

As Mary's fourth sorrow breaks into her world, may we search into
her heart and learn the lessons that she learned, to experience the joy
that she lived.

---

27   https://www.youtube.com/watch?v=rd9UD2psUH8&list=RDrd9UD2psUH8&start_radio=1

28   Pope Francis, Evangelii Gaudium, n. 286.

WHY WAS THE ENCOUNTER WITH JESUS ON THE WAY TO CALVARY A SWORD IN MARY'S HEART?

For nearly three years, Mary has been mostly home alone. Her little boy has blossomed into a strong man, confident, independent, and traversing the Judean countryside, stirring inspiring stories wherever he goes. When he told her his plan to head out to the desert for 40 days of prayer and fasting, like Moses (Ex 24:28) and Elijah (1 Kings 19:8) before him, she tried to pack some things in his satchel, but he just smiled and left it behind. During those 40 days she kept her own vigil, casting aside the clouds of worry about the dangers facing her son—poisonous snakes, scorpions, predatory animals, bandits, scorching heat, thirst, and hunger—and mulling over the significance of his choice to follow in the footsteps of the greatest leader of the Jewish people who received the Law, and the greatest prophet who returned his people to the God of the Law. She prayed, interceded, contemplated. Her heart was gradually embracing the mission of her son.

Friends brought back stories of seeing Jesus healthy and whole on the banks of the Jordan. They'd seen him with his cousin, John. That was consoling. Though he wasn't with her, at least he was with a relative, even if it was John, who'd been acting a bit wild the past few years, not settling down into a profession and marriage, but instead dressing in coarse attire, subsisting on whatever food he could scrounge up, and stirring up trouble with King Herod. Okay, John perhaps wasn't exactly the most popular of their relatives, but Mary knew his heart was in the right place, and that he certainly was making a name for himself.

What consolation it had been to see Jesus come home a few weeks later! And not just Jesus, but his new friends, too. A rough and tumble bunch, to be sure—and boy, could they drink! At the wedding feast in Cana, they'd helped to finish off the wine, and Mary had gently told Jesus that the hosts had run out. "Do whatever he tells you," she had told the servants (John 2:5). And Jesus had made her so proud that day! He fixed the situation, he showed his power, he worked a miracle, and he began his mission.

Yet even in all the happy news and events, there had been a twinge of sadness, of detachment.

During his public life [Mary] had to step aside, to make
place for the birth of Jesus's new family, the family of
his disciples. She also had to hear the words: "Who is
my mother and who are my brothers?... Whoever does
the will of my Father in heaven is brother, and sister and
mother." Mt 12:48–50 Now we see her as the Mother
of Jesus, not only physically, but also in her heart. Even
before she conceived him bodily, through her obedience
she conceived him in her heart.[29]

The past two years had passed by so quickly. For periods of time she
had been able to accompany Jesus and his new disciples on some of
his shorter trips to the neighboring villages, but more often than not
she just heard the stories from others. She picks up on the growing
excitement around her son, but also the augmenting animosity. She
sensed the tension, the mounting expectation. She heard the questions,
"Who is this Jesus? Is he the Messiah?" (Mt 16:13) "By whose
authority is he healing the sick and blind and lame and casting out
demons?" (Mark 11:28) "Where did this man get all this?" (Mark 6:2)
"Can anything good come from Nazareth?" (John 1:46) She smiles
upon hearing these questions, glowing with the insights of personal
experience and contemplation that cannot be transmitted except
by one's own encounter with her Son. Yes, his mission as Messiah
is developing splendidly, and more disciples are added with each
multiplication of loaves, each division of sin, and each subtraction of
suffering.

This past Sabbath had brought things to a climax. The crowds shouting
hosannas to the son of David had whipped up expectation in Jerusalem
to a fever pitch. Her own heart was soaring. Would this be the moment
for him to manifest himself to the whole people? Would he now carry
out the work of redemption? Could this be the moment for him to be
lifted up in glory (cf. John 12:32)?

Forebodings creep into her heart, though, too. She knew the prophet
Isaiah's words about the suffering servant (cf. Is 53). She had heard Jesus
say, "And when I am lifted up from the earth, I will draw everyone to
myself" (John 12:32). She wondered what he meant about "being lifted

---

29   Joseph Cardinal Ratzinger, Via Crucis, 2005.

up." Surely that must have been him being lifted up the donkey for his triumphal entrance into Jerusalem. Or was there more to come? She'd heard firsthand how Jesus challenged his disciples saying, "Whoever wishes to come after me must deny himself, take up his cross, and follow me. For whoever wishes to save his life will lose it, but whoever loses his life for my sake will find it" (Mt 16:24–25). Surely that was figurative—or was it?

Then comes that terrible night. Jesus was out with his friends for the Passover Seder. Mary turned in early after the fatigue of travelling to Jerusalem for the feast days, only to be rudely awakened by frantic cries about arrest and torches and swords, and disciples betraying her Son and escaping naked, and a rushed illegal trial by night. All is confusion and turmoil, outside and inside. What's going on? Where's her son? What are they doing to him? Can they really be so blind as to not see who he is?

Mary's worst worries are becoming real. The contrast with just a few days ago is so stark. Her hopes—along with those of so many others— are being crushed beneath the heel of Pharisaical wounded pride and Sadducaical pragmatic self-serving cynicism, while Roman "justice" perpetrates the gravest injustice in human history.

Mary rushes to the Sanhedrin and then the Praetorium. Brief glimpses through the crowd and muffled fragments of conversation give her a chaotic perspective on all that is transpiring. But she senses the rejection, the mob hatred for her Son, starkly contrasted with her own maternal and filial love.

Jesus is pushed through a side door by the guards, only to reemerge bruised, battered, and spattered with blood. A regal crown releasing red rivulets mixes into the now-crimson garment she had woven white for him. She sees her son suffering, rejected, and with no escape. He's abandoned by his friends, and the fickle crowds are now crying out for Barabbas. Can this really be happening? Could God be asking of her what he asked of Abraham, to sacrifice a beloved son (cf. Gen 22:1–19)? In his case, God had provided a ram instead. But hadn't Jesus been called the "Lamb of God" (cf. John 1:29 and 1:36)? It dawns on her that this time will not be like the opposition he faced in Nazareth, when he simply walked away through the mob with his quiet authority. This time, he's

Antonio Ciseri, Ecce Homo, 1871, Galleria dell'Arte Moderna, Florence, Italy, https://vidalcuglietta.com/ecce-homo-painting/121331/ecce-homo-painting-best-of-ecce-homo-by-antonio-ciseri/.

not walking away. He's not going to show his power. And she has no power to help him. If she could, she'd do whatever it takes to save him, but there is nothing. And worst of all, she has no chance to console him, to be with him, to bind up his wounds, to protect him from further harm. Every fiber in her motherly being aligns with his pain.

He is disfigured, beaten, bloody, marring all the beautiful memories she had treasured in her heart. New brutal memories crowd out everything beautiful. Barking Roman soldiers force the prisoners to take up their crosses. From a raised doorstep across the street, Mary's eyes seek out Jesus, but his eyes are embracing the Cross. Surely this could not be what he meant when he said, "take up your cross and follow me" (Mark 8:34). What was he doing? When would he end all this madness?

The crowd continues to sneer and jeer, hurling insults at the prisoners and Roman soldiers equally, pressing in on all sides. Mary can't penetrate. She just wants to walk beside Jesus, to be with him, to caress him, but even that consolation is kept from her. The brusque guards shove her son and keep the throngs at bay, relentlessly forcing the death march up the narrow stone street towards the place of crucifixion. Yet

Raphael, Il Spasimo, 1514, Museo del Prado, Madrid. https://upload.wikimedia.org/wikipedia/
commons/7/70/Raphael_Spasimo.jpg

perhaps worst of all is the indifferent curiosity of onlookers who take her and her son's suffering as their entertainment.

Every motherly instinct in Mary drives her to reach out to her son, to touch him, to protect him from more hurt, to embrace and console him. Yet there is even more at work here than a mother's instinct: there is an important lesson of faith for every follower of Jesus in this fourth sorrow of Mary, as suffering son and sorrowing mother meet on the Way of the Cross. In this encounter, we uncover something of the "theology of encounter" that is beginning to emerge in the Catholic world, especially during the papacy of Pope Francis.

In common English usage, the term "encounter" most often refers to a chance meeting, coming across someone unexpectedly, happenstance. It's something superficial and passing.[30] The way this term is utilized in Catholic theology is decidedly different. There are three levels to the Catholic usage.

1. At the first level, it draws upon the existentialist philosophical insights of Søren Kierkegaard (1813–1855), Martin Buber (1878–1965), and others. Encounter here refers to interpersonal discovery, awakening, understanding, love, compassion, and awareness of the other person as a person. Encounter is a dawn: new light breaks across the horizon of understanding and I become aware that the person before me is not an obstacle or threat, not a thing, not a means to my ends. Pope Francis, commenting on a passage from the book of Genesis, describes it in this way: "The original Hebrew suggests a direct encounter, face to face, eye to eye, in a kind of silent dialogue... It is an encounter with a face, a 'thou,' who reflects God's own love."[31] At this first level, encounter is a discovery of the person before me and of that person's dignity in God, an awakening of love.

The Regnum Christi Member Handbook points out the importance of this encounter:

30 As a verb, Google defines it as: "unexpectedly experience or be faced with (something difficult or hostile)" and synonyms include: experience, hit, run into, come up against, face, be faced with, confront. As a noun, Google defines it as "an unexpected or casual meeting with someone or something" and the synonyms are meeting or chance meeting.

31 Pope Francis, *Amoris Laetitia*, n.12

> *The human person was not created to live in solitude.*
> *Love is mankind's essential calling or vocation. Only*
> *in love, that is to say in the gift of himself, can man*
> *discover the truth of his own being. As Pope John Paul*
> *II wonderfully declared, man "remains a mystery*
> *to himself; his life is without meaning unless love*
> *reveals itself to him, unless he* **encounters** *love, unless*
> *he experiences and assimilates it, unless he actively*
> *participates in it.*[32]

2. The second level of encounter entails discovering God as person. For so many, God is an idea, a remote concept, or an abstract theory of origins or causality. Conceiving of God in that way leads to practical atheism in everyday life, because God is distant and not relevant for one's day-to-day decisions and aspirations. For religion to be relevant, there must be more; an encounter with the living God—Father, Son, or Holy Spirit—is the only power that can ignite faith and authentic spirituality. God is not distant from us, because in the Son he is Emmanuel, God-with-us, who took on our human condition and our punishment.

Pope Benedict XVI places encounter at the core of Christianity: "Being a Christian is not the result of an ethical choice or a lofty idea, but the encounter with an event, a person, which gives life a new horizon and a decisive direction" [emphasis added][33]. The encounter with Christ— with a Jesus who is not just a historical figure, a prophet, wise man, or teacher... but a Jesus who is real, alive, and loves me personally—is the beginning of real life.

The encounter with Christ shakes up people's priorities precisely because it opens new potential, fresh possibilities. A personal experience of who Jesus is and how he loves me transforms timorous disciples of mediocre talent into fearless missionaries. Pope Francis states it beautifully:

32   Regnum Christi Member Handbook, n.3.

33   Pope Benedict xvi, *Deus Caritas Est*, n.1.

*Thanks solely to this encounter—or renewed
encounter—with God's love, which blossoms into
an enriching friendship, we are liberated from our
narrowness and self-absorption. We become fully
human when we become more than human, when we
let God bring us beyond ourselves in order to attain
the fullest truth of our being. Here we find the source
and inspiration of all our efforts at evangelization.
For if we have received the love which restores
meaning to our lives, how can we fail to share that
love with others?*[34]

This experience of life-changing love—of God who is Love—
is the foundation of our drive to evangelize, as the Regnum
Christi Member Handbook so aptly states:

*The mission stems from a deep, personal experience:
your living and life-changing encounter with Christ.
The apostle extracts not only the content but also the
certainty and enthusiasm of his missionary activity
from this encounter, which he matures in faith,
nourishes in hope, and gives life to in love. More
than structures and programs, the mission needs
men and women who have experienced God's love
in their own lives and feel called to work tirelessly to
proclaim and extend his Kingdom using every licit
and good means until Jesus Christ reigns in the hearts
of men and societies.*[35]

The Blessed Virgin Mary—more than any human being—
encountered Jesus in this way, and because of that encounter
and embracing of her mission, has borne the title "Queen of
the Apostles."

3.   Many theologians would stop at the second level, but I consider
     that there is a third—and perhaps deepest—level of encounter.
     It's the moment when doubting Thomas finally recognizes who

Jesus is by probing his wounds, and he cries out, "My Lord and my God!" (cf. John 20:27–29) It's the level of mystics, of saints, of those who enter intimacy with God beyond human categories. This is what the Virgin Mary experiences on the Way of the Cross. She already had a level of familiarity with Jesus that exceeded what we can ever dream about; now Jesus introduces her to the gift he reserves for those he loves the most: his Cross.

Archbishop Luis Martínez highlights this gift in his book *Secrets of the Interior Life*: "The supreme gift of the love of Jesus to souls is sorrow and the cross; for the supreme gift of the love of souls is this very cross that contains all the treasures of heaven and earth, since it embraces all the riches of love."[36]

Humanly speaking, the first two levels of encounter are appealing because we discover love that fills our hearts and souls, and meaning that gives orientation to our life. The third level appears humanly repulsive. No sane person desires pain or likes suffering. When we witness it, our natural reaction is to turn away, like the prophet Isaiah says of the suffering servant, "one of those from whom men hide their faces" (Is 53:3). We find it repulsive in others and fear it for ourselves.

But "perfect love drives out fear" (1 Jn 4:18).

It is the nature of love to transform those who love, to the point of uniting them one to another in a certain manner. The words, 'to have but one heart and one soul,' are not mere hyperbole; they express a mystery of unity that all love achieves, since it effects that those who love one another have the same thoughts and the same affections, that their joys and their sorrows are shared in common.[37]

---

36   Archbishop Luis M. Martínez, *Secrets of the Interior Life*, p. 70. He goes on to say, "In the life of love there are three great stages: the first prepares for union, the second consists in the union itself, and the third contains the prodigious consequences of this union which continues and grows more perfect. And to each of these three stages there corresponds a sorrow, or rather, a whole class of sorrows."

37   Archbishop Luis M. Martínez, *Secrets of the Interior Life*, p. 68.

It is precisely this richness of love that enables Mary to overcome her fear of the soldiers, the opposition of the mob, and the gory specter of Jesus beaten and bruised to encounter him on the Way of the Cross. She goes beyond the call of a mother. She embraces the suffering of her Son in a way that opens her own life to sorrow, not as an evil to be shunned, but as a path to redemption.[38] In this way, "suffering, a consequence of original sin, acquires a new meaning; it becomes a participation in the saving work of Jesus."[39]

> *Encounter that brings us into the pain of our neighbor,*
> *that unites us with the Passion of Christ, is redemptive.*
> *This is not simply a fatalistic acceptance of sorrow*
> *and our lot in life, passively throwing up one's hands*
> *and saying, "whatever." No! Redemptive encounter is*
> *to do as the Virgin Mary did, actively embracing her*
> *Son who is sorrow, who through obedient suffering*
> *redeems. "Through his suffering, my servant shall*
> *justify many, and their guilt he shall bear"*
> *(Isaiah 53:11).*

When we embrace our daily crosses with love, we, too, contribute to Christ's work of salvation. As St. Paul stated so eloquently, "in my flesh I am filling up what is lacking in the afflictions of Christ on behalf of his body, which is the church" (Col 1:24). This is a profound mystery, that our pains offered in love can compare with Christ's, can contribute to salvation.

Our Blessed Mother is the first to discover and participate in Christ's redemptive suffering, right here on the road to Calvary. Later, Peter would say it in this way:

> *"What credit is there if you are patient when beaten*
> *for doing wrong? But if you are patient when you*
> *suffer for doing what is good, this is a grace before*
> *God. For to this you have been called, because Christ*
> *also suffered for you, leaving you an example that you*
> *should follow in his footsteps."*
> *1 Peter 2:20–21*

---

38   For a deeper consideration of redemptive suffering, the following article provides good insights. http://www.religious-vocation.com/redemptive_suffering.html#.WSAZRWjyu00

39   Catechism of the Catholic Church, n.1521.

Mary was first to follow in his footsteps, literally and spiritually. You and I have been called, too, to take up our cross and follow him.[40] Inside, many of us cringe when we hear those words. Our imagination goes to the discomfort and pain, we worry about future implications, and we shy away from the cross, preferring the simple mediocrity of a bystander hanging around the edges of Jesus's followers, but afraid to commit. In so doing, we completely miss the deepest level of encounter with Jesus, which means we miss the best of love, fulfillment, and joy.

MARY'S SORROW TRANSFORMED INTO JOY

> *Come, all you who pass by the way, look and see*
> *whether there is any suffering like my suffering, which*
> *has been dealt me.*
> *Lamentations 1:12*

The most intense sorrows of Mary have begun, yet as we have already discovered, suffering also opens up the possibility of deeper joys. How did the Virgin Mary allow God to transform into joy the pain of witnessing her Son's suffering? With Simeon's prophecy she had learned to overcome worry by reflecting on the past, living the present, and trusting in God's Providence for the future. During the flight into Egypt, she learned to let go of all the things people put their trust in instead of God. At the loss of Jesus in the Temple, she had learned to cast out all fear through perfect love and develop a new and deeper relationship with Jesus.

But those lessons cannot cope with this new sorrow. God the Father of mercies has more for her—and for us—to learn. Faced with the brutal manhandling of her Son and the injustice of imminent execution, evil seems to have gained the upper hand. It makes no sense. She cannot fathom the hows, the whats, the whys. It is all jumbled together in one confusing mess of anguish.

1. The Virgin Mary shows us that one of the secrets to taking up our cross and unlocking joy is in the encounter. If we focus

---

40   Cf. Matthew 10:38-39 "Whoever does not take up his cross and follow after me is not worthy of me. Whoever finds his life will lose it, and whoever loses his life for my sake will find it." See also Mt 16:24, Mark 8:34, Luke 9:23.

on the suffering, we balk; if we focus on Jesus, we can do everything (cf. Phil 4:13). Just ask Peter, who walked on water as long as his eyes were on Jesus (cf. Mt 14:28–31). Close to his heart, we can experience calm amid chaos, joy during suffering. This is the strange paradox once again: sorrow can open us up to joy. That's why St. Paul was able to say, "I rejoice in my sufferings"[41] and St. Peter affirms, "Rejoice to the extent that you share in the sufferings of Christ, so that when his glory is revealed you may also rejoice exultantly" (1 Pt 4:13).

2. In addition to learning the "theology of encounter" at its deepest level, Mary is learning through this sorrow that her Son is "making all things new" (Rev 21:5). She recognizes that he has embraced his Cross—literally—and that he has chosen this path of redemption, that he wants his Father's will and our redemption more than he fears death or desires life. That is PASSION! Mary glimpses something of the bigger picture: the silent lamb led to slaughter (cf. Is 53:7, Acts 8:32). The Lamb of God who takes away the sins of the world. A new Passover, a new covenant is on the horizon. All these things she perceives dimly, in the light of faith. By faith, we too can begin to see on the dark horizon of pain and suffering a hint of the Son-rise's rays.

3. We love only to the degree that we are willing to suffer. Precisely because Mary encounters Love and faith enables her to see beyond the present moment, her sorrow on the streets of Jerusalem teaches us a third lesson as she learns it from her Son: *embrace the cross*.[42] The saints experienced this paradox in their own lives, so much that St. Thomas Aquinas could affirm that "All the saints who have pleased God have gone through many tribulations by which they were made the sons of

---

41   Col 1:24, see also 2 Cor 1:5 "Christ's sufferings overflow to us, so through Christ does our encouragement also overflow" and Phil 3:8-10 "For his sake I have accepted the loss of all things and I consider them so much rubbish, that I may gain Christ and be found in him, not having any righteousness of my own based on the law but that which comes through faith in Christ, the righteousness from God, depending on faith to know him and the power of his resurrection and (the) sharing of his sufferings by being conformed to his death."

42   In *The Imitation of Christ*, the spiritual classic of Thomas à Kempis, Book 2, Chapter 12 is entitled *On the Royal Road of the Holy Cross*. This poignant text states better than I ever could what the Virgin Mary teaches us through this fourth sorrow. I highly recommend reading and meditating on this beautiful text.

God."[43] St. Padre Pio experienced the sweetest joys in suffering and came to desire it, not because he was a masochist, but because through it he grew in love.[44] St. Faustina Kowalska discovered that, "From the moment I came to love suffering, it ceased to be a suffering for me."[45] How is that possible? Because she found what Mary found on the Way of the Cross: an encounter with Jesus on the deepest level, the level that leads to the profoundest intimacy and union, the level where sorrow is transformed into joy.

---

43   St. Thomas Aquinas, *Commentary on Hebrews*. See also an excellent article on with an insightful perspective on suffering: http://www.calledtocommunion.com/2009/08/a-catholic-reflection-on-the-meaning-of-suffering/.

44   Gianluigi Pasquale, Secrets of a Soul: The Letters of Padre Pio to his Spiritual Fathers, October, 2003. "When Jesus wants me to understand that He loves me, He allows me to savor the wounds, the thorns, the agonies of His passion...When He wants to delight me, He fills my heart with that spirit which is all fire; He speaks to me of His delights. But when He wants to be delighted, He speaks to me of His sorrows, He invites me—with a voice full of both supplication and authority— to affix my body [to the cross] in order to alleviate His suffering. Who can resist Him? I realize how much my miseries have caused Him to suffer, how much I have offended Him. I desire no other than Jesus alone, I want nothing more than His pains (because this is what Jesus wishes). Let me say— since no one can hear me—I am disposed to remain forever deprived of the sweetness Jesus allows me to feel. I am ready to suffer Jesus hiding His beautiful eyes from me, so long as He does not hide His love from me, because then I would die. But I do not feel I can be deprived of suffering—for this I lack strength. [...] Perhaps I have not yet expressed myself clearly with regards to the secret of this suffering. Jesus, the Man of Sorrows, wants all Christians to imitate Him; He has offered this chalice to me yet again, and I have accepted it. That is why He does not spare me. My humble sufferings are worth nothing, but Jesus delights in them because He loved [suffering] on earth...Now shouldn't this alone be enough to humiliate me, to make me seek to be hidden from the eyes of men, since I was made worthy of suffering with Jesus and as Jesus? Ah, my father! I feel too keenly my ingratitude toward God's majesty."

45   Diary of St. Maria Faustina Kowalska, Notebook 1, n.276.

QUESTIONS FOR PERSONAL REFLECTION OR DISCUSSION

1. Do I follow Christ because the crowds of people around me call out "Hosanna!" to him, or because I have encountered his love for me at a deeper level?

2. When I face shame for his name, do I pretend not to know him, or do I push through the crowds to accompany my Lord wherever he may go?

3. When I experience the burden of family members or friends whose mistakes and messy lives seem to drag me down, how do I turn to the Virgin Mary and to Jesus Christ for strength? Do I walk away from tough situations? How can I love as Christ calls me to love?

4. In what ways have I embraced my cross? How have I experienced the joy that comes from uniting my suffering with Christ?

5. How do I show that I truly believe that Jesus can "make all things new," and that even apparent failure and defeat can be turned into glory for those who trust in the Lord?

6. When I feel weak or that I cannot go on, do I ask the Holy Spirit for the gift of fortitude?

AN INVITATION TO PRAYER

Dear Mother Mary, as the pains of motherhood turn into the sorrow of solitude, help me to walk alongside your Son as you did. Life is messy, and you did not find your consolation and joy in having everything work out according to your plans, but in embracing God's plan. Deepen my trust in God the Father. Strengthen my awareness of Jesus by my side as I take up my cross each day to follow him. Inflame my heart with the Holy Spirit's love, so that his gift of fortitude may make me strong in the face of every temptation to love less, to stop short, to bail out of difficult situations. Blessed Mother, teach me how to love better! Amen.

Hail Mary full of grace …

Jesus, I trust in you!

CHAPTER 5

JESUS DIES ON THE CROSS

"Standing by the cross of Jesus were his mother and his mother's sister, Mary the wife of Clopas, and Mary of Magdala."
John 19:25

Andrea Mantegna, Crucifixion, 1457–1459, The Louvre. Paris, France.

SACRED MUSIC TO AID CONTEMPLATION

◇ *Stabat Mater*[46]

◇ *Crown of Thorns* by Danielle Rose[47]

◇ *My God, My God* by the Consecrated Women of Regnum Christi[48]

---

46   https://www.youtube.com/watch?v=4US4PSZF278

47   https://www.youtube.com/watch?v=5JG0ZpiRRhQ

48   This song can be found on the CD "Discovering God's Love for You" at https://store.
      missionnetwork.com/collections/regnum-christi-store/products/discovering-gods-love-for-
      you?variant=7711322931242.

THE PROXIMITY OF DEATH CHANGES LIFE

Immediately before I began preparing this reflection on the fifth sorrow of the Blessed Virgin Mary, I suffered a heart attack. At 39 years of age and in good health, the last thing I expected was to have 100% blockage of my right coronary artery.

Many people have asked me what God taught me through the experience. I think I will be mulling that over for the rest of my life, but four things have become very clear for me so far. Each of them has led to slowing down the frenetic pace of my life, encountering others at a deeper level, and learning the art of accompaniment:

1. *The importance of prayer.* A week into my convalescence, a friend sent a note and said that she had woken up early the morning of my heart attack, and felt prompted by the Holy Spirit to intercede for me. She didn't know why she was praying for me at that moment, and I didn't know that she was praying, but God knew. The time had been 5:30 a.m., exactly when I was arriving at the emergency room. Intercessory prayer is powerful.

2. *Wisdom from my big sister.* My oldest sister, Vicki, is a doctor and wanted to know all the details of what had happened, the symptoms, the procedure, the medication I was on and dosage levels. I fed her the information she sought, and then she texted to me that I needed to slow down. I texted back: "It's really hard to slow down." Her reply: "I sympathize. Sometimes it takes a big event to reset our view on how much we need to take personal responsibility for and when we need to have the humility to accept that others are just as capable as we are. And if you or I die next week, the world will figure out how to go on without us." It's a good lesson to learn.

3. *Acceptance of the love, appreciation, and service of others.* This is hard for us, especially for me because I am very proud, and I don't like to accept help or expressions of love. But I have had to learn how to let myself be helped, accompanied by others, and loved by other people. In a sense, what has happened to me physically has also happened to me spiritually: allowing myself to be loved and allowing my heart to be healed.

4.   *Learning how to express better the love that is in my own heart.* As I entered surgery, the superior of my community called my parents to advise them of my heart attack. I talked with my mom shortly after surgery. I was groggy, explaining as best I could what had happened. At the end of the conversation, she said, "I love you and we are going to try to drive and come to visit with you." My parents lived ten hours away in Northern Arkansas. I replied, "I don't want to inconvenience you, Mom. If you can't come, don't worry about it, but I love you too." When my parents arrived at the hospital the next morning, she wanted to talk with me personally, so she kicked everyone else out of the room and said to me, "Fr. Daniel, you know over the years that you have been in the seminary and as a priest you have always been so tough and distant, and you never told me that you love me. Yesterday was the first time that you said, 'I love you' in decades." Scenes from the years of non-expression flashed before my eyes, the pain in her heart at not hearing it from me, the regret and sorrow she felt as her son nearly died. My heart softened. I pushed aside the IV tubes and wires stringing from my chest to embrace her. We cried together. My heart was healing on more levels than one.

SILENCE SALUTES SORROW

The sorrow of a mother with her dying child silences all chatter. We tiptoe in timorousness, afraid to venture a word, to make a sound. There are no appropriate words at this moment. Respectful silence is the only way to contemplate such a scene. "Where love is concerned, silence is always more eloquent than words."[49]

That is the challenge of this meditation on the fifth sorrow of the Blessed Virgin Mary. We gaze upon the Blessed Mother in her sorrow and do not know what to say or where to begin. Tears, an embrace, perhaps a reassuring squeeze of the hand—but no words.

These last four sorrows of Mary surrounding the passion and death of her Son draw us deeply into the mystery of encounter and accompaniment. In her heart, the motherly desire to protect, heal, console, and accompany is tested by trepidation. She wants to be by his side, yet she fears. What will happen to her? He's an adult now, shouldn't she let go and just live her own life? Like the parents of the blind man, she perhaps feels the temptation to go her own way, leave the cross, and say, "He's of age; he can speak for himself" (cf. John 9:21). As with the parents of every drug addict, prisoner, or special-needs child, the temptation to cut ties and move on with one's own life is very real.

Yet, "can a mother forget her infant, be without tenderness for the child of her womb" (Is 49:15)? King Solomon in his wisdom recognized the power of maternal instinct, and that a mother is ready to do whatever it takes to save her own child, even if it means relinquishing her claim to him (cf. 1 Kings 3:16–28), or taking the blow of the sword instead: "A sword will pierce through your own soul" (Luke 2:35).

> [Mary] then recall[s] the words of the prophets, words like these: "He was oppressed, and he was afflicted, yet he opened not his mouth; he was like a lamb that is led to slaughter" (Is 54:7). Now it all takes place. In her heart she had kept the words of the angel, spoken to her in the beginning: "Do not be afraid, Mary" (Luke

---

49   Pope Francis, Amoris Laetitia, n.12.

*1:30). The disciples fled, yet she did not flee. She stayed
there, with a Mother's courage, a Mother's fidelity, a
Mother's goodness, and a faith which did not waver
in the hour of darkness: "Blessed is she who believed"
(Luke 1:45). "Nevertheless, when the Son of man
comes, will he find faith on earth?" (Luke 18:8). Yes,
in this moment Jesus knows: he will find faith. In this
hour, this is his great consolation.*[50]

Mary recognizes that she cannot change all the circumstances and save
her Son, but she can do something. She can accompany him.

More than any other human being, the Blessed Virgin Mary
encountered her Son Jesus Christ, and so more than anyone else
she was able to accompany him in life and death. She knows him as
only a mother can know her son. Every quirk, every thought, every
motivation. At the foot of the Cross, she draws other women who have
experienced the life-transforming love of her Son into this ministry of
accompaniment.

50   Joseph Cardinal Ratzinger, Via Crucis, 2005.

HOW DID JESUS' DEATH PIERCE MARY'S HEART?

We take a moment now to stand quietly next to Mary, to see what she sees, hear what she hears, and feel what she feels as Luke relates the scene in his Gospel:

> *When they came to the place called the Skull, they crucified him and the criminals there, one on his right, the other on his left. Then Jesus said, 'Father, forgive them, they know not what they do.' They divided his garments by casting lots. The people stood by and watched; the rulers, meanwhile, sneered at him and said, 'He saved others, let him save himself if he is the chosen one, the Messiah of God.' Even the soldiers jeered at him. As they approached to offer him wine they called out, 'If you are King of the Jews, save yourself.' Above him there was an inscription that read, 'This is the King of the Jews.'*
> *Luke 23:33–38 (see also Matthew 27:33–54, Mark 15:22–39, and John 19:23–30)*

Mary looks on the scene. There's really nothing she can say, nothing she can do. She sees his humiliation, stripped of his clothing and his human dignity, no longer preaching and powerful, but suffering, dying. She resists the temptation to despair, to let the hope in God's promises die in her heart as she sees the Messiah expiring on the Cross. She feels the temptation to wonder if she hasn't been deluded this whole time. But she latches on to the words whispered during the Last Supper: "So you also are now in anguish. But I will see you again, and your hearts will rejoice, and no one will take your joy away from you" (John 16:22). For now, she accompanies; she watches; she weeps.

In the silence of her heart, Mary must have gone back to the words of the prophet Jeremiah: "Why did I come forth from the womb, to see sorrow and pain, to end my days in shame" (Jer 20:18)? Mary struggles to take it all in. Too much, too fast, too brutal. At moments like this, you simply stumble forward in a daze. You watch, and you see, as she did, that:

> *When the soldiers had crucified Jesus, they took his clothes and divided them into four shares, a share for*

> *each soldier. They also took his tunic, but the tunic*
> *was seamless, woven in one piece from the top down.*
> *So they said to one another, 'Let's not tear it, but cast*
> *lots for it to see whose it will be,' in order that the*
> *passage of scripture might be fulfilled (that says): 'They*
> *divided my garments among them, and for my vesture*
> *they cast lots.' This is what the soldiers did."*
> John 19:23–24

Mary looks on the scene as the executioners who tortured her son now toss dice to take his tunic. She had woven it herself. It was the fruit of hours and days of loving labor, and now these rough hands, hurtful hands, the hands that execute jealousy and injustice, take it as booty. She resists the temptation to anger and resentment. She had every "right" to hate these men, and not only them, but also the disciples who abandoned him, the Jewish leaders who handed him over, Pilate in his cowardice—but instead Mary chooses to follow her Son, forgiving. "Father forgive them, they know not what they do" (Luke 23:34). She doesn't exercise her rights or retain any rancor; she enters the realm of forgiveness.

> *Standing by the cross of Jesus were his mother and his*
> *mother's sister, Mary the wife of Clopas, and Mary of*
> *Magdala.*
> John 19:25

Mary of Magdala. Here stands another woman whose life was transformed by an encounter with Jesus. I think this is why Mary of Magdala is one of the few disciples of Jesus who makes it to the foot of the Cross. She had already tasted death, the barrenness of a life of sin away from Christ, and she was not afraid to risk everything to stay with Jesus, her life. She was loved, she had been touched by him, she was redeemed by him. Nothing else mattered. Those who have encountered Jesus understand this.

ACCOMPANYING JESUS

Shortly after my heart attack, I had a profound spiritual experience in
the Holy Land at Magdala, hometown of this same Mary who stands at
the foot of the Cross with the mother of Jesus.

In 2004, when Pope John Paul II entrusted the Vatican's place in the
Holy Land—the Notre Dame of Jerusalem Center—to the Legionaries
of Christ, Fr. John Solana recognized that a dwelling for pilgrims to
pray and stay was needed in Galilee. He started searching for land to
buy for this new center, and soon found a piece of property right on
the Sea of Galilee, at the foot of Mt. Arbel, near where the ancient city
of Magdala[51] was located. The town had been destroyed by raiding
Romans ca. 67 AD and then soon after was covered by a landslide. It
was never rebuilt, and for nearly two millennia it remained buried. A
run-down hotel and bar, pasture for sheep, and weeds covered the site.

Fr. Solana envisioned a chapel, a hotel for pilgrims, and a restaurant
on the newly acquired plot. According to Israeli law, however,
archeological digs must be conducted before construction of new
buildings. As they began the excavations, a first-century synagogue, a
menorah stone, and the ancient village of Magdala were unearthed.[52]
This turned out to be one of the greatest archaeological finds in the
state of Israel in recent years.

Ever since the original discovery in 2007, excavation and construction
continued on the site, and now the "Duc in Altum" center is open "for
worship, Mass, and prayer for people of all faiths." This beautiful
place sparks reflection and brings the imagination back to the times of
Jesus. The altar is shaped as a ship, a boat just like the one that Jesus
would have sailed in with his disciples. The mast forms the cross of
the altar, and the glass windows behind look out across a mirror pool
to meld into the waters of the Sea of Galilee. All around the center are
mosaics of women—just like Mary of Magdala—who encountered
Jesus and experienced his love, mercy, and redemption. This Mary of
Magdala was by most accounts a great sinner, fallen into the greatest

51   https://en.wikipedia.org/wiki/Magdala

52   http://www.magdalaproject.org/WP/?langswitch_lang=en. See also http://www.magdala.org/visit/
     archaeological-park/the-magdala-stone/.

Photo taken by Fr Daniel Brandenburg in Magdala Center, Israel.

of disrepute, yet was restored by Christ and elevated to the great
dignity of being his disciple and a first witness to his Resurrection.

The new pilgrim center at Mary of Magdala's old hometown is
beautiful, but what really struck me was beneath the building. I was
searching for a restroom, and as I walked down the stairs the open
space of a small chapel to my left caught my eye. I peered into the room,
noting the gray pavement stones from the original city streets, quite
probably where Jesus himself walked. My eyes strode across the rough
stones to the back wall, where a 12'x7' convex painting caught my eye.

Across the canvas were the feet and lower legs of a group of men,
walking on stones like those of the chapel floor. Gray pavement stones,
dirty feet, rough sandals, a staff—and one hand. An old woman's hand.
A hand reaching out to touch the edge of Jesus's garment. The woman
who for 12 years hemorrhaged blood, and in this moment, is healed by
touching. The artist depicted this moment of encounter by an orb of
light right around that fingertip.

Other pilgrims from our group found their way to this hidden chapel.
No one told them to stay, but each one was captivated by the scene that
had drawn me in, and spontaneously each one began to pray. Someone
suggested that we pray the rosary together. We finished the rosary, but
no one got up to leave. We just sat there in contemplation, and pilgrims
started to share insights and reflections on the moment the woman
touches the garment of Jesus, and the healing power that came from
him, and how each of the sacraments are the moments when Christ
touches us. In the artist's rendition, the halo around the touch looks like

the Eucharistic host, with power emanating forth. We stayed there for an hour. For me, it was the most powerful encounter on that pilgrimage to the Holy Land, a moment when we touched Jesus, when we were touched by him.

"His mother and his mother's sister, Mary the wife of Clopas, and Mary of Magdala" (John 19:25) were all there at the foot of the Cross because they had encountered Jesus. John, "the disciple whom Jesus loved" (John 19:26), was there because he had encountered Jesus. We will stay with Jesus only insofar as we have encountered him.

The Blessed Mother's love and the Holy Spirit's gift of fortitude enabled her to make it to the foot of the Cross. As she looks up at the fruit of her womb suspended by spikes in his hands and feet, what is it that holds her up? What is it that sustains her? What does she see? John relates it in his gospel:

> When Jesus saw his mother and the disciple there whom he loved, he said to his mother, "Woman, behold, your son." Then he said to the disciple, "Behold, your mother." And from that hour the disciple took her into his home.
> John 19:27

In a reflection on this scene in The Joy of the Gospel, Pope Francis says:

> On the cross, when Jesus endured in his own flesh the dramatic encounter of the sin of the world and God's mercy, he could feel at his feet the consoling presence of his mother and his friend. At that crucial moment, before fully accomplishing the work which his Father had entrusted to him, Jesus said to Mary: "Woman, here is your son." Then he said to his beloved friend: "Here is your mother" (John 19:26–27). These words of the dying Jesus are not chiefly the expression of his devotion and concern for his mother; rather, they are a revelatory formula which manifests the mystery of a special saving mission. Jesus left us his mother to be our mother. Only after doing so did Jesus know that "all was now finished" (John 19:28). At the foot

James Tissot, What Our Lord Saw from the Cross (Ce que voyait Notre-Seigneur sur la Croix),
1886–1894, Brooklyn Museum, New York.

> *of the cross, at the supreme hour of the new creation,*
> *Christ led us to Mary. He brought us to her because he*
> *did not want us to journey without a mother, and our*
> *people read in this maternal image all the mysteries of*
> *the Gospel. The Lord did not want to leave the Church*
> *without this icon of womanhood. Mary, who brought*
> *him into the world with great faith, also accompanies*
> *"the rest of her offspring, those who keep the*
> *commandments of God and bear testimony to Jesus"*
> *(Rev 12:17).*[53]

Mary underwent a difficult exchange at the foot of the Cross. Standing there, Jesus said to her, "Behold your son" (John 19:26). She trades her perfect son, the son of God, for John. This John who was a sinner, a "son of thunder" (Mark 3:17), scheming and ambitious (Mt 20:21–27), imperfect in so many ways. We know John is a saint today because of his adopted mother. In that exchange, Mary also acquired us. What headaches we must give our spiritual mother! We come with our complaints, our whining, our imperfections. But she loves it. She loves us, accompanies us, and excels at lifting us up to holiness in her Son. The exchange - from Jesus to John, from one Son to all of humanity - was an elevation: not only is she the Theotokos (Mother of God), but she has become the mother of all humanity. Suffering prepared her heart to embrace all of us in our imperfections and misery.

Mary is the model for the whole Church, and she shows us how to suffer in faith and charity, yet with hope.[54] The writer of the letter to the Hebrews wrote, as if he had learned it from the Virgin Mary's own lips: "At the time, all discipline seems a cause not for joy but for pain, yet later it brings the peaceful fruit of righteousness to those who are trained by it. So strengthen your drooping hands and your weak knees. Make straight paths for your feet, that what is lame may not be dislocated but healed" (Heb 12:11–13).

---

53   Pope Francis, *Evangelii Gaudium*, n. 285.

54   Catechism of the Catholic Church, n. 967. "By her complete adherence to the Father's will, to his Son's redemptive work, and to every prompting of the Holy Spirit, the Virgin Mary is the Church's model of faith and charity. Thus she is a 'preeminent and . . . wholly unique member of the Church'; indeed, she is the 'exemplary realization' (typus) of the Church."

Mary sorrows. As we read in Scripture, "There is no sorrow like unto my sorrow" (Lam 1:12). Yet her sorrow is not self-pity. She channels the sorrow into accompaniment of her Son, and by the will of Jesus her accompaniment has become accompaniment of us all. She has become the mother of all Christians, of all who suffer. She knows the depths of sorrow and she knows how to be with us, how to console us, to unite our suffering to her Son, to make sense of our tribulations. She is our mother. She is my mother.

> *It was now about noon and darkness came over*
> *the whole land until three in the afternoon because*
> *of an eclipse of the sun. Then the veil of the temple*
> *was torn down the middle. Jesus cried out in a loud*
> *voice, 'Father, into your hands I commend my spirit';*
> *and when he had said this he breathed his last. The*
> *centurion who witnessed what had happened glorified*
> *God and said, 'This man was innocent beyond doubt.'*
> *Luke 23:44–47*

We cannot fix all the problems in our world, but we can accompany others in their sorrows. The suffering of a mother in seeing her dying child is the greatest of sorrows. Yet even here, in this deepest distress, we learn that death can become life, darkness turns into light, and sorrow can be transformed into joy.

MARY'S SORROW TRANSFORMED INTO JOY

I think there are three lessons that we can learn from the Blessed Virgin Mary, at the foot of the Cross.

1. Authentic love emboldens us to accompany others even in the darkest moments. In the deepest sorrow, there are often no logical answers. We can accompany and walk alongside the one we love. We cannot remove the evil or change the circumstances, but we can be there to support and love. We can learn the "art of accompaniment" that Mary lived, and that Pope Francis has urged all Catholics to practice.[55] There is joy in simply accompanying her Son. It is sorrow and joy simultaneously. Authentic love always co-exists with both sorrow and joy, because joy is a fruit of charity and sorrow is deepest where love is widest. Mary is there at the foot of the Cross; she doesn't have to say anything, she doesn't have to do anything. She's not saving him from his pain and suffering, but the fact that she is there is significant. That's one of the lessons I learned in the hospital; I told my mother not to bother coming because I didn't want to inconvenience her. But my mom was there; she was not going to listen to my silly comments about not inconveniencing her. She wanted to be with me in the hospital, not because she could fix my heart, not because she could give tips to the cardiologist or nurses, not because she could take away the pain, not because she could do my rehab for me, but just to show her love. Being there for those that we love is sometimes of the greatest importance. It can also be our greatest joy. Let us not flee from suffering. Let us not turn away from the difficulties and problems in our life. Be there for those that you love.

---

55 Pope Francis, *Evangelii Gaudium*, n. 169-173. "In a culture paradoxically suffering from anonymity and at the same time obsessed with the details of other people's lives, shamelessly given over to morbid curiosity, the Church must look more closely and sympathetically at others whenever necessary... Although it sounds obvious, spiritual accompaniment must lead others ever closer to God, in whom we attain true freedom. Some people think they are free if they can avoid God; they fail to see that they remain existentially orphaned, helpless, homeless. They cease being pilgrims and become drifters, flitting around themselves and never getting anywhere. To accompany them would be counterproductive if it became a sort of therapy supporting their self-absorption and ceased to be a pilgrimage with Christ to the Father."

2. We can learn from the Blessed Virgin Mary's willingness to accept a new son (John), a new family (all Christians), and a new mission (Mother of the Church). Some of the greatest fears I've seen in women's hearts are that of openness to a new child, to new in-laws, and to a new apostolate they are asked to begin. It is so easy to give in to fear. Mary shows us the internal attitude that conquers fear and leads to blessedness. She was there at the foot of the Cross only for Jesus, yet her divine Son has more in store for her. In his last words, "Woman, behold your son," her mission is amplified. She embraces the newness and the greatness graciously, generously. How beautiful is it to know that we have a heavenly mother who cares for us, who watches over us. Even if our earthly mother is imperfect or no longer here, we have a mother who loves us and cares for us, who is always there for us, who is always ready to listen to us and to bring our prayers and petitions before her Son. A generous, open heart that never says "no" to Jesus: that is what leads to joy.

3. We can learn from the Blessed Virgin Mary to recognize— through faith and hope—the saving mission of her Son even during the sorrow. Pain makes us myopic. The intensity of our sorrow tends to blind us to the bigger picture, to the things that are going quite well, and to the possibilities that the future holds. Mary does not let the pain put blinders on her. Faith doesn't lessen her sorrow at the death of Jesus or the pain that is in her heart, but it does allow her to look beyond the here and now, to see past the suffering and brutality and violence of the cross, and recognize in it redemption and salvation and a completion of the Father's plan. Mary teaches us how to look beyond our own short-sighted vision of reality and recognize what God's plan is in the midst of our pain and suffering. Let us pray for an increase of our faith and hope.

QUESTIONS FOR PERSONAL REFLECTION OR DISCUSSION

1. How do I usually react when others hurt me or those I love? Why? Do I hold on to anger and resentment, or forgive as Jesus did on the Cross, as Mary did at the foot of the Cross?

2. In what ways do I live out the importance of prayer of intercession for others? How do I respond when the Holy Spirit leads me to pray for someone?

3. How do I accept the love and appreciation of those around me? Do I let others accompany and console me or do I have walls built up in my mind or heart?

4. How do I express my love for others in words and deeds? In what ways do I accompany others and console them in their sorrows?

5. What aspects of the "art of accompaniment" have I assimilated in my own life? What elements do I need to continue developing, with God's grace?

6. Have I embraced the Blessed Virgin Mary as my mother? How could I ask her for the help I need to follow Jesus and be his disciple?

AN INVITATION TO PRAYER

Dear Blessed Mother, there is no sorrow like your sorrow, looking upon your son Jesus as he dies. Move me beyond curiosity; shake me out of my dull indifference. Help me to recognize the depth of Jesus's love for me, shown in every blow of the whip, in each bloody footstep, at every fall of the hammer driving in the nails, as he is lifted up, at each tortuous breath, in every word he utters in those last moments. Mary, move my heart! Let it beat in unison with your Immaculate Heart! Let it be pierced with His Sacred Heart! Let me love as you love, let me love what you love!

Hail Mary full of grace...

Jesus, I trust in you!

CHAPTER 6

JESUS IS PIERCED WITH A LANCE AND LOWERED FROM THE CROSS INTO MARY'S ARMS

"He was pierced for our offenses, crushed for our sins… When he was cut off from the land of the living, and smitten for the sin of his people, a grave was assigned him among the wicked and a burial place with evildoers … Through his suffering, my servant shall justify many, and their guilt he shall bear."
Isaiah 53:5–11

James Tissot, What Our Lord Saw from the Cross (Ce que voyait Notre-Seigneur sur la Croix),
1886–1894, Brooklyn Museum, New York.

SACRED MUSIC TO AID CONTEMPLATION

◇ Serenata Triste by Eric Genuis[56]

◇ Show Me by Audrey Assad[57]

Why do we reflect on the seven sorrows of Mary? Left up to our natural inclinations, we'd all rather avoid difficulty and discomfort, flee from the specter of sorrow in our lives. We'd prefer to turn away from the dark moments, the shadows, and leave pain behind, so that we simply experience joy and happiness and never-ending delight. That is what our human nature desires.

So why is it that in Catholic tradition we reflect on the seven sorrows of Mary? I hope that these pages have made the answer clear: by embracing our cross and following Christ, the inescapable sorrows of every human life can be transformed into deep joy. We cannot eliminate suffering, but we can find meaning in it.

A few years ago, I met a good man named Jack.[58] He was sitting one balmy summer evening with his wife on their porch swing, enjoying the sunset and a cool breeze, when the chain broke and they both tumbled to the deck. His wife brushed herself off and got right up, but he had fallen awkwardly, shattering vertebrae and leaving him partially paralyzed. For months, he was in the hospital with the broken back and a special neck brace, and endured multiple surgeries to repair his spine. The week after his accident, I went to the hospital to celebrate Mass for him. After Mass, we chatted for some time and prayed together. Jack was seeking St. Andre Bessette's intercession for healing and restoration to full health, so he could continue providing for his family. He was a man of deep faith, quite accomplished in the business world, a good husband and father. I remember sensing then that God was not going to give him a miraculous healing, but rather he was giving him the gift of his cross—that gift that he reserves for those whom he loves the most.

---

56   https://www.youtube.com/watch?v=XsLsxe4WlvE
57   https://www.youtube.com/watch?v=z2ZBCUQieUI
58   Not his real name.

I prayed with him there in the hospital room saying, "Let's ask not so much for healing, but for God's will."

Some years after that initial hospital visit, Jack sought me out for spiritual direction. He was in his wheelchair, still paralyzed from the waist down. During the intervening time since the accident, he had recovered very little mobility and lost financial security. Dependence on those around him for the simplest tasks was his daily bread. One of his sons had taken a hiatus from university studies to help, but a year later, for no clear reasons, that young man took his life. So, as I visited Jack, he was struggling with his misfortunes, his own limitations, that God hadn't healed him, mourning the one-year anniversary of his son's suicide, and feeling guilt: Did he cause this? Was he too hard on his son? What more could he have done?

On top of all these calamities, his atheist nephew had been arguing with him that God doesn't exist. How could God allow so much suffering in the world? "You've been in a wheelchair; all these good things have been taken away from you. How could a good God exist?" The woes had piled up to become a wall blocking his vision, and in his darker moments Jack's thoughts coincided with the taunts of his nephew.

When we spoke that day, Jack broke down. It's hard to see a man cry, because you know there is a deep well of sorrow there. But as we spoke, he already knew in his heart that God was blessing him through the afflictions. He jokingly said he was going to change his name from Jack to Job. As his worldly securities and pleasures had fallen away, his spiritual life and meaningful relationships had deepened. Talking through it all, he was able to reflect once again on the blessings that God was showering on him, precisely through the cross. At one point I said, "After my heart attack, one of the hardest things for me was to let people love me, to let myself be taken care of, not to have to fend for myself and do everything myself, but to allow myself to be loved." He nodded his head and said, "That's really hard."

We cannot eliminate suffering in this life, but we can find meaning in it when we encounter Jesus Christ. Through that encounter with God who is love, we accompany and are accompanied, authentic joy fills our hearts, and even death itself becomes the doorway to life. Our ultimate bliss is not in this world, but in the life to come. These spiritual truths are what we discover in the sixth sorrow of the Blessed Virgin Mary, as she stands at the foot of the Cross and sees her son dead, now pierced with a lance and lowered from the cross into her arms.

HOW DID THIS SIXTH SORROW PIERCE MARY'S HEART?

For the past several hours, Mary has been dragged through a surreal landscape of pain, her life crumbling around her. She awakens into a bad dream: Jesus arrested, the disciples' flight, the farce of justice perpetrated by her own Jewish leaders and the Roman authorities, the flagellation of her son, his bloody footprints on the path to Calvary. For the past three hours, she has hovered around the site of the Crucifixion, drawing as close to the Cross as the guards will allow. She can do nothing but accompany her son, near his bloodied feet. He cries out with his last breath, and she exhales with him, the tears blazing trails through the blood and dust caking her face.

At a moment like this, a mother should be left alone in silence to grieve, to take the time she needs to weep and mourn. But the soldiers are in a hurry to finish get this business.

> *Now since it was preparation day, in order that the bodies might not remain on the cross on the sabbath, for the sabbath day of that week was a solemn one, the Jews asked Pilate that their legs be broken and they be taken down. So the soldiers came and broke the legs of the first and then of the other one who was crucified with Jesus. But when they came to Jesus and saw that he was already dead, they did not break his legs, but one soldier thrust his lance into his side, and immediately blood and water flowed out. An eyewitness has testified, and his testimony is true; he knows that he is speaking the truth, so that you also may (come to) believe. For this happened so that the scripture passage might be fulfilled: "Not a bone of it will be broken." And again another passage says: "They will look upon him whom they have pierced."*
> *John 19:31–37*

Pierced, out of love for us. As Mary stands with her tear-streaked face upturned to her Son on the Cross, the full weight of her Son's life trajectory hits her. He had foretold this. The prophets had foretold this. "They shall look upon him whom they have pierced" and "I will pour out … a spirit of grace and petition" the prophet Zechariah had declared 500 years before the birth of Jesus (Zec 12:10).

Mary knew the scriptures, all the prophecies. In the shadow of the Cross, she ruminates on them. Jesus had said, "When I am lifted up from the earth, then I will draw all people to myself" (John 12:32). What madness was this? The barbarous cruelty of this Cross was shameful and revolting; and his friends had abandoned him, the Jewish leaders repudiated him, and the guards scorned him. How was he drawing people to himself? Yet there was something more in that prophecy. Something that Mary was still formulating in her heart, intuiting that more was yet to come. Yes, we naturally shy away from suffering, yet we are also drawn toward love, and no greater love has any man than to lay down his life for a friend (cf. John 15:13). Was this what Jesus was doing? Showing us a love so great that none could remain indifferent? Giving us a trophy of the triumph of love over evil and hatred?[59]

---

59   St. John Chrysostom has a poignant homily *On the Burial Place and the Cross* that draws out this victory of the Cross: "Have you seen the wonderful victory? Have you seen the splendid deeds of the Cross? Shall I tell you something still more marvellous? Learn in what way the victory was gained, and you will be even more astonished. For by the very means by which the devil had conquered, by these Christ conquered him; and taking up the weapons with which he had fought, he defeated him. Listen to how it was done. A virgin, a tree, and a death were the symbols of our defeat. The virgin was Eve: she had not yet known man; the tree was the tree of the knowledge of good and evil; the death was Adam's penalty. But behold again a Virgin and a tree and a death, those symbols of defeat, become the symbols of his victory. For in place of Eve there is Mary; in place of the tree of the knowledge of good and evil, the tree of the Cross; in place of the death of Adam, the death of Christ. Do you see him defeated by the very things through which he had conquered? At the foot of the tree the devil overcame Adam; at the foot of the tree Christ vanquished the devil. And that first tree sent men to Hades; this second one calls back even those who had already gone down there. Again, the former tree concealed man already despoiled and stripped; the second tree shows a naked victor on high for all to see. And that earlier death condemned those who were born after it; this second death gives life again to those who were born before it. Who can tell the Lord's mighty deeds? By death we were made immortal: these are the glorious deeds of the Cross. Have you understood the victory? Have you grasped how it was wrought? Learn now, how this victory was gained without any sweat or toil of ours. No weapons of ours were stained with blood; our feet did not stand in the front line of battle; we suffered no wounds; witnessed no tumults; and yet we obtained the victory. The battle was the Lord's, the crown is ours. Since then victory is ours, let us imitate the soldiers, and with joyful voices sing the songs of victory. Let us praise the Lord and say, Death is swallowed up in victory. O death, where is thy victory? O death, where is thy sting? The Cross did all these wonderful things for us: the Cross is a war memorial erected against the demons, a sword against sin, the sword with which Christ slew the serpent. The Cross is the Father's will, the glory of the Only-begotten, the Spirit's exultation, the beauty of the angels, the guardian of the Church. Paul glories in the Cross; it is the rampart of the saints, it is the light of the whole world." From Office of Readings, Saturday Memorial of the Blessed Virgin Mary, The Divine Office I: Advent, Christmastide, and Weeks 1-9 of the Year.

And then she sees that they go to break the legs of the criminals hanging beside Jesus, but they do not break a single one of his bones. She remembers that prophecy, the reference to the Passover lamb (cf. John 19:36, Ex 12:46). Everything is coming to fulfillment. It might be the end for Jesus, but it's a new beginning for those who follow him.

This was her Son. His lifeblood streamed out along the staff of the spear, spilling to the ground, spattering upon the bystanders. "A fountain shall be opened for all" (cf. Zec 13:1).

St. Peter's Basilica in Rome has four huge statues around the main baldacchino, and one of them is of Longinus. The massive statue nearly 15 feet tall depicts this Roman soldier standing with lance in hand, the spear he thrust into the side of Jesus. There is a longstanding tradition that bathed in the blood and water of the redeemer, he became a believer. He experienced the darkness of life without Christ, and through the Cross of Christ came to believe: "Truly this man was the Son of God!" (Mark 15:39) His conversion reminds us that every ending is the possibility of a new beginning.

Gianlorenzo Bernini, San Longino, 1631–1638, St Peter's Basilica, Vatican City.

St. Bernard of Clairvaux sums up the scene's significance: "The Heart of Jesus was wounded, that through the visible wound, the invisible wound of love might be seen."[60] As Jesus's side is pierced with a lance, drawing out water and blood, the source of the sacraments is tapped and the Church flows forth.

The Virgin Mary—until the moment Jesus's death is confirmed by the thrust of the lance—was still wondering, hoping: Maybe he would come down from the cross. Maybe this nightmare would end. Maybe the soldiers would just disappear, and the chief priests and the scribes would stop their mockery and have a conversion of heart and come to realize that her son was the son of God, that he was come to save them, and maybe his disciples would suddenly appear from out of the crowd and say, "Lord, we are sorry that we betrayed you, we are sorry that we ran away in fear. Here we are." And maybe he could have pulled out those nails, or in a blast of light and power come down from the Cross and displayed to all the people present that he was indeed the Messiah. But no, he is dead. His life gone. It is definitive.

The nails are extracted from his hands and feet, and his broken body lowered down from the Cross. As she gathers him into her arms, the blood and spittle, the serum which ran out of his heart, the flies and bits of gravel from his falls cover his mangled body and now hers. He becomes part of Mary. The blood spattered and now clotting releases a peculiar odor. Mary is not inhibited by any of it. She takes Jesus into her arms; she holds him.

James Tissot, The Descent from the Cross (La descent de croix), 1886, Brooklyn Museum, New York.

William-Adolphe Bouguereau, Pieta, 1876, Dallas Museum of Fine Arts.

St. Peter's Basilica in Rome houses another marble sculpture that is arguably the greatest masterpiece by the greatest sculptor of all time, Michelangelo. The Pietà captures this moment of Mary's sorrow as she holds the body of her Son. Spend time here to contemplate the emotions of Mary.

William-Adolphe Bouguereau, Pieta, 1876, Dallas Museum of Fine Arts.

Mary is tempted to despair. A mother faced with the death of her child should be allowed to mourn, to stay quiet, to simply be with her son. But instead everything is rushed. The soldiers just wanted to get the job done. She is not allowed to mull over the wonderful years they spent together. The chief priests and scribes want to expedite the execution, so they can observe the Sabbath. What sorry hypocrisy! A spear is run through Jesus to ensure that he is dead. They take him down quickly from the cross. Mary's memories are mangled. What sticks in her mind is not the beautiful memory of Jesus in her arms after his birth, nursing at her breast, but instead the image of his bruised, battered, and bloodied body staining her clothes, his limp and lifeless form.

Mary is rushed in her grief. She is not able to take the time to hold her son as long as she would like, to give him a proper burial. They arrange aromatic herbs and anoint his body with a little bit of oil, then quickly wrap a linen shroud around him. That's it. They stick him into Joseph of Arimathea's tomb and depart.

Darkness blots out the beauty of the years spent with Jesus.

The temptation to despair becomes deafening in the silence. The silence in which her son speaks no more, and in which God says nothing. The Jewish leaders are gone, and they say nothing. The guards are finished with their job; they are somber, they are scared. They had cried out: "Truly this man was the son of God," (Mark 15:39) but now they say no more. John the apostle, her new son, is in shock and isn't saying anything. Mary is left in this void, with no words of consolation. The silence of God contrasts with the pained cries of her heart.

Abandoned and alone. Where are all Jesus's friends? John is there, and Joseph of Arimathea is skulking nearby (John 19:37–38). But where are the rest of the twelve Apostles? The thousands who cried out just a week ago, "Hosanna to the son of David" (Mt 21:9), where are they? Where are the five thousand who were fed by Jesus in the multiplication of the loaves (Mark 6:44)? It seems as if everyone has forgotten favors and friendship in the face of failure. Yet not all. Some women stand by the foot of the Cross (John 19:25); this offers dim consolation.

Mary also faces fear of the future. Her mind races with uncertainty, because now her Son, her mainstay, the last of her remaining close relatives is gone. Who is going to care for her? Yes, John, he is her son now. Supposedly he will take care of her.

These temptations to despair and unbounded grief are topped by the darkest thought yet: to prefer giving up, losing the will to live. When I spoke with Jack, the man in a wheelchair whose son committed suicide, he said honestly: "Father, I kind of wish sometimes that I hadn't just broken my vertebrae but had died, because I am such a burden to my wife." It's hard to give voice to those dark thoughts that can come sometimes into our heart, when we wonder, "Wouldn't it have been better if I hadn't lived?" And Mary may have experienced that temptation as well, the dark temptation to lose the will to live. She, too, is human, not divine.

Holiness does not mean that we never experience temptation. Holiness does not mean that we are not human or that we don't feel and experience passions in our own heart. Holiness means to transform the sorrow, the passions, the darkness—through faith in God—into light. It's Mary's internal attitudes that bring God's light into the dark places, overcoming the temptations.

MARY'S SORROW TRANSFORMED INTO JOY

What are the four attitudes that the Blessed Virgin Mary likely adopted at this moment to transform these deepest of sorrows into joy?

1. Mary allows herself to grieve. The prophet Zechariah had foretold this moment when he wrote, "When they look on me, on him whom they have pierced, they shall mourn for him, as one mourns for an only child, and weep bitterly over him, as one weeps over a firstborn" (Zec 12:10, cf. John 19:37). Sometimes we don't want other people to see our tears. We don't want other people to see that something is a deep struggle for us, so we try to hide it or put on a mask. Jack told me, "Father, a lot of times people ask me how I am doing. I just lie to them. I tell them, 'I am doing great. I feel really good. Today is a good day.' But, inside there is doubt, hatred of the situation, frustration." Lies never liberate; the truth makes us free (John 8:32). We must allow ourselves to grieve properly. That's what Jesus did (John 11:35). Can we doubt that Mary did the same? She pours out her tears. She empties her heart and grief upon the bruised body of the Son in her arms.

2. The second attitude of Mary is simple: just stay with me. She accompanies in silence, even in death. A love as strong as death, said Solomon (cf. Songs 8:6). To accompany those that we love, even in death, is an act of love. It is something that soothes the heart and is part of the grieving process. Mary teaches us not to turn away our face from death, but to open our heart to the deeper reality that God wants to teach us through death. This is what will burst forth from the Resurrection of Christ. Death is not the end. Death does not have the final say, because her Son will triumph over death. In that moment as she holds her Son, wraps him in the shroud, she feels all the darkness. But even then, in accompanying her son she is beginning to look forward to the power of his Resurrection.

3. Here emerges the third of Mary's internal attitudes. She savors the good memories (cf. Luke 2:19), all the while building new relationships. She doesn't stay stuck in the pain of the past. Her new son, John, is entrusted to her and she nurtures this

innovation in their relationship. As we see in the first chapter
of the Acts of the Apostles, Mary is with the disciples. She is
there as their mother, leading them in prayer, teaching them
how to pray. She is bringing them together, helping them
overcome their difficulties and rifts, helping them see things
with faith. These same things, the Blessed Virgin Mary helps
us to do today. She helps us to look beyond our difficulties, to
see through sorrow into that which is to come. To see into life.
To see during our struggles that God has a better plan. That he
has a plan that is bringing us to salvation. By savoring the good
memories and recalling in gratitude all the good that God has
done, she can recognize the blessings and a path forward. She
resists the temptation to despair. Like her, we all feel at times
the temptation to despair, to doubt, to lack of faith. Resisting
those temptations and coming out on the other side of it makes
us better, makes us stronger. In this moment, Mary latches onto
hope—hope that she begins to see the disciples around her: the
centurion who cried out, "Truly this man was the son of God";
John, who was strong and stayed at the foot of the Cross; and
Joseph of Arimathea, who finally found the courage to come
out and publicly take a stand for Christ. All these examples of
faith are little pinpoints of light piercing the darkness.

4.   A fourth attitude is displayed in Mary's piety. Each one of
     Mary's sorrows is providentially paired with one of the seven
     gifts of the Holy Spirit. Here at the foot of the Cross we see
     the gift of piety, or in Italian "pietà," the name given to the
     artistic renditions of the Blessed Virgin Mary holding onto
     the broken body of Jesus. St. Thomas Aquinas describes piety
     as the reverence for God that leads us to work good for all,[61]
     while Pope Francis makes clear that "piety is not mere outward
     religiosity; it is that genuine religious spirit which makes us turn
     to the Father as his children and to grow in our love for others,
     seeing them as our brothers and sisters."[62] This piety is a gift of
     the Holy Spirit. When we look at Mary holding Jesus, it stirs
     up in our hearts reverence for something sacred, a moment of

---

61   Cf. St. Thomas Aquinas, Summa Theologiae, I-II, q.68, art.4, ad.2.

62   Pope Francis, Discourse at the General Audience, June 4, 2014.

sorrow, a moment of great intimacy. Piety does not end with
pity (i.e. inward-looking absorption in sadness), but rather
reverent recognition of God's goodness that leads us to bring
his love to everyone around us. Piety spurs us to share the gift.

This reflection on Mary's attitudes leads us to suggest six questions
about our own attitudes:

QUESTIONS FOR PERSONAL REFLECTION OR DISCUSSION

1. How have my personal sins wounded the heart of Jesus,
   perhaps more than the soldier's lance ever did?

2. What do the saints see in the blood and water coming from
   Jesus's side that I still need to grasp more deeply in my own life?
   The totality of Christ's self-giving love? God's mercy flowing
   out to heal humanity? The birth of the Church? The source of
   the sacraments?

3. How do I handle rejection, silence and grief in my own life?
   Do I flee from it? Does it embitter my heart, stirring anger,
   resentment, or close-heartedness? Do I lose perspective? Or do
   I process grief in the same faith that the Virgin Mary showed at
   the foot of the Cross?

4. How can I better foster gratitude and hope in my heart? How
   can I encourage it in others?

5. What are some instances where I have recognized signs of hope,
   conversion, and rebirth even in dark situations? Do I base it on
   merely a cheerful disposition, or on a profound faith, hope, and
   love that come from prayer and communion with Jesus Christ?

6. What differences could the Holy Spirit's gift of piety
   make in my life?

AN INVITATION TO PRAYER

Virgin Mary, Mother of Sorrows, you experienced the deepest depths
of human sorrow. You watched rough soldiers not satisfied with killing
your Son, but even after death desecrating his body with the blow of a
lance through the heart. He could not feel that anymore, but you did.
As you held his bloodied corpse in your arms, you resisted temptations
to despair and unbounded grief. You latched onto hope in his promises.
You stirred up gratitude for his life and remembrance of the good he left
behind. You recognized the redemptive power of his sacrifice for our
sins. Without the night, we'd never see the beauty of the stars. Mary,
help me to see like that! Mary, help me to love like that! Show me how
to trust, to hope, to forgive! Do not let my heart drown in sorrow, but
lead me always to a deeper faith in your Son, Jesus Christ.

Hail Mary full of grace ...

Jesus, I trust in you!

CHAPTER 7

JESUS IS BURIED
IN THE TOMB

"Amen, amen, I say to you, you will weep and mourn, while the world rejoices; you will grieve, but your grief will become joy. When a woman is in labor, she is in anguish because her hour has arrived; but when she has given birth to a child, she no longer remembers the pain because of her joy that a child has been born into the world. So you also are now in anguish. But I will see you again, and your hearts will rejoice, and no one will take your joy away from you."
John 16:20–22

The Entombment of Christ, Galleria Borghese, 1610 https://en.wikipedia.org/wiki/Sisto_Badalocchio#/
media/File:Sisto_Badalocchio_-_The_Entombment_of_Christ,_1610.jpg

SACRED MUSIC TO AID CONTEMPLATION

◈ Holding On by the Consecrated Women of Regnum Christi[63]

◈ Hallelujah by Kelley Mooney[64]

◈ Time to Say Goodbye by Andrea Bocelli[65]

◈ Arise by the Consecrated Women of Regnum Christi[66]

◈ Even unto Death by Audrey Assad[67]

---

63   https://www.youtube.com/watch?v=d1x7ysFxYPg

64   https://www.youtube.com/watch?v=hZi3ut9ee0Y

65   https://www.youtube.com/watch?v=4L_yCwFD6Jo

66   https://www.youtube.com/watch?v=RMYjx6U44v0

67   https://www.youtube.com/watch?v=aETZ6ETKAtI

HOLDING ON, LETTING GO

Over the years, I have been to many funerals and cemetery interments, but one stands out in my memory. Regina Grace Chmiel was born April 11, 2015, with a list of physical ailments too long to enumerate here, and miraculously hung onto life until just short of her first birthday. Her obituary recounts, "Regina lived her short life to the fullest and traveled extensively, taking 12 flights in 9 months! She visited Spain, California, and Ohio, and saw both the Atlantic and Pacific Oceans."[68]

Already in the womb, the doctors informed Regina's parents that her life would not be easy or long. They expected her to die within hours of childbirth. Where some saw a pointless existence, however, her parents saw a beautiful gift. "Through her beautiful example, we encountered the grace and mercy of God. To know Regina was to witness the mystery and dignity of human life, and God's particular love for each soul."[69]

On February 11, 2016, St. Francis de Sales Parish in Lebanon, Ohio, was packed for the funeral, but the next day for the interment at Gate of Heaven cemetery, there was only immediate family, two funeral home officials who maintained a respectful distance, and me. Six lonely figures stood out among the rolling hills of gravestones, braving that bleak, blustery winter day. As Regina's parents carried her little casket to the graveside, I understood more deeply that the loss of a child is the greatest sorrow for a parent. Tears flowed freely, and even after the ceremony, they seemed unable to pull away from the graveside, despite the biting breeze. Moving on with life, letting go of the past—even with the greatest of faith, this is easier said than done.

Another mother, dealing with the death of a child, wrote this insightful phrase: "I wonder… if the rent in the canvas of our life backdrop, the losses that puncture our world, our own emptiness, might actually become places to see. To see through to God."[70]

The Blessed Virgin Mary's seventh and final sorrow is the burial of her Son in the tomb. It's been a strangely beautiful path for us. We have

---

68   http://www.legacy.com/obituaries/dayton/obituary.aspx?pid=177650945

69   Idem.

70   Ann Voskamp, One Thousand Gifts, p. 22.

entered into the sorrows of the Blessed Virgin Mary knowing that
through them we are not mucking in the misery, but through them we
are coming into a deeper joy. There is no human life without sorrow.
We all experience travails, miseries, difficulties, sad moments, and
frustrations; that's just part and parcel of human life. But the beauty of
looking at the life of the Blessed Virgin Mary is to see how she was able
to transform her sorrows—which when you look on the scale of things
were very significant—into the greatest of joys.

> *One of the most important things in the spiritual life*
> *is to understand well the intimate relations between*
> *love and sacrifice... When we come to understand*
> *that perfection consists in love, and that this love*
> *is attained, conserved, and consummated only by*
> *sacrifice, then we have found the path of sanctity.*[71]

This is what we have been learning from Mary. Through the first six
sorrows, we've learned from her how to deal with worry, rejection, loss,
and fear; how the encounter with Jesus deepens our love and allows us
to accompany those who suffer; and how to forgive. So now we reflect
on the seventh and final sorrow: Jesus is buried in the tomb.

HOW DID THE BURIAL OF CHRIST IN THE TOMB PIERCE MARY'S HEART?

We have accompanied the Blessed Mother along this path of pain: her
Son was arrested, scourged, and sentenced to crucifixion. She meets him
along the Way of the Cross. He's nailed to the Cross and she stands at
the foot of the Cross. We saw with her the spear driven into the side of
Jesus, piercing through his heart, blood and water flowing out. Then
he is taken down from the Cross and placed into her arms. "They shall
look on him whom they have thrust through, and they shall mourn for
him as one mourns for an only son, and they shall grieve over him as
one grieves over a first-born" (Zec 12:10).

So how was the burial of Christ a sorrow for Mary? What greater
sorrow could possibly exist than what we've already witnessed?

71   Archbishop Luis M. Martínez, *Secrets of the Interior Life*, B. Herder Book Co., St. Louis, 1949.
      Page 59-60.

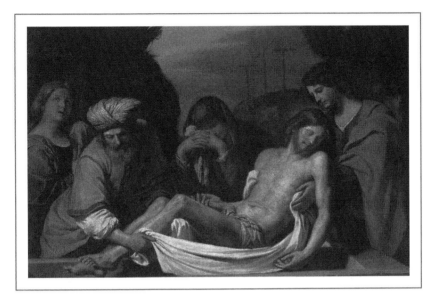

Guercino, The Entombment, c. 1656, The Art Institute of Chicago, https://www.artic.edu/
artworks/86323/the-entombment?q=the+entombment.

Why would there be any more grief beyond what she has already experienced? Wouldn't his burial be a relief, the cessation of suffering, an end to the misery?

I think there is a reason why there is this seventh sorrow of Mary, because in placing her Son in the tomb and wrapping him in the shroud, she traded that linen garment she wove for him for a burial shroud. I have always been fascinated by the Shroud of Turin. During my years of study in Italy, I also was able to see the Shroud of Manoppello, the Sudarium Christi. The Shroud of Turin is that linen cloth that covered the entire body of Jesus; the Shroud of Manoppello was a cloth that was placed just on the face of Jesus. These shrouds contain clues to the story of Christ's suffering, his death and resurrection.[72]

She exchanged her divine Son for an imperfect son, John, and imperfect children, each one of us. There is a transfer taking place in her life, coming to this moment where she has to say goodbye, a definitive goodbye, a letting go.

---

72   More detail can be found at https://en.wikipedia.org/wiki/Shroud_of_Turin.

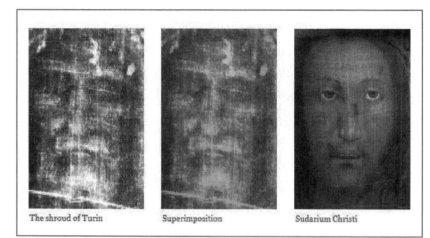

The shroud of Turin   Superimposition   Sudarium Christi

Overlay of photographs from the Shroud of Turin and the Sudarium Christi, copyrighted by Sr. Blandina Paschalis Schloemer.

This is what distinguishes this sorrow from the preceding ones: the definitive nature of the loss. Whatever God has in store, she will never be able to go back to the way things were before, at Nazareth, with Jesus there. She has to release that, to allow herself to accept that loss, in order to receive the new gift God wants to give. This is not easy. And when we are faced with detachment in our own lives, Mary shows us the way.

At the moment she feels utterly spent, with nothing more to give. She has endured the greatest suffering a mother can experience. And now others are turning to her for strength, when she feels none at all. John is there, trying to hold it together. And Mary Magdalene is there, and she is weeping, and the others are turning to her as if she is the strong one, but she doesn't feel any strength of her own. All she wants at this moment is time to mourn. She recalls the words of the prophet Jeremiah, "Mourn for him, all you his neighbors, all you who knew him well! Say: How the strong staff is broken, the glorious rod!" (Jer 48:17)

It is time to weep. "Avoid not those who weep, but mourn with those who mourn," says the wise man in Sirach 7:34. It is time to be alone, to have the solitude necessary to properly grieve. This moment, stirs up the memories of another burial, when a few years back she had to bury Joseph. Joseph, who did not rise from the dead. It was a definitive goodbye. And the temptation creeps into her heart of losing any sliver of hope.

She doesn't have the time she wants to hold her son and to weep upon him. The sabbath is coming and the soldiers are rushing to get them out of there and Joseph of Arimathea is encouraging her to wrap his body, saying, "Let's go, we have to move on." There's no time to give him the proper burial, to go through the necessary rites, to anoint his body properly. Her grief is rushed. And then she starts to think about the place she has to bury her son, not in Nazareth, not even in Bethlehem, but in Jerusalem, a place far from her home. How is she going to be able to visit his tomb? She won't be able to visit his grave in the future except when she returns for the feasts.

All these mumbles and jumbles in her mind, all these confused thoughts and stress and all this going on, with no support. The disciples, the ones who had been Jesus's closest companions, where are they? They are not there, they have jumped ship. There is John, but only John; one of twelve, one of five hundred. Where are the others? Even the crowds that had lingered around the Cross as Jesus died, making fun of him, they've dispersed, too. Everyone's gone.

Perhaps one of the deepest sorrows and pains is that there are no apologies, no condolences, from anyone. The chief priests and scribes don't come back and say, "Oh, Mary, we are so sorry that we did this to your son; we were so mistaken." No, there is the dark silence. There's no asking for forgiveness. There was no repentance. There's only the body of her son being wrapped in the shroud. Being taken away from her. And Mary has to experience detachment. For 33 years, Jesus has been the center of her existence. He's been her everything. What now?

You know, I think our world gets things so backwards sometimes. We put so much insistence upon our freedom, upon our autonomy, upon our free time, our ability to do what we want. We put so much stock in that autonomy, as if that were the source of our happiness and fulfillment. But it's not. Our happiness comes not from being detached and alone, but in being united with others. It comes from loving and being loved and feeling needed and needing others. It comes from that beautiful interplay of interdependence.

Joseph Ratzinger, in *Introduction to Christianity*, spoke about the relationship that leads to unity, specifically within the Trinity. The Trinity is not three isolated individuals; the unity of relationship between the three persons is the substance of God. And God is love. It's a profound reflection. We are made in the image and likeness of God; we are not made to be isolated individuals all on our own. We are made to love. We are made to be with others. Our happiness comes not from being alone, but from being united. Loving others, being cared for *and* caring for. Freedom is not the defining characteristic of human life, but rather interdependence, relationship, love.

Perhaps that's why in his last words from the Cross, Jesus seeing his mother, gave her a new son to care for, to ease the passage, to ease the transition. "Behold your son." She must learn to navigate a new relationship, a new role in her life. "Blessed are they who mourn, for they will be comforted," Jesus had said in Matthew 5:4. Mary is comforted by John. She experiences the fulfillment of the messianic prophecy uttered by Isaiah:

> *I will heal them and lead them; I will give full comfort*
> *to them and to those who mourn for them, I, the*
> *Creator, who gave them life. Peace, peace to the far*
> *and the near, says the LORD; and I will heal them.*
> *Isaiah 57:18–19*

For this her Son had come: not just to suffer, but to bring redemption and peace; not merely to die, but to transform sorrow into joy. At the synagogue in Nazareth in the first days of his ministry, he stood up to read the prophecy of Isaiah that explained his mission:

> *The spirit of the Lord GOD is upon me, because*
> *the LORD has anointed me; he has sent me to bring*
> *glad tidings to the lowly, to heal the brokenhearted,*
> *to proclaim liberty to the captives and release to the*
> *prisoners, to announce a year of favor from the LORD*
> *and a day of vindication by our God, to comfort all*
> *who mourn.*
> *Isaiah 61:1–2*

MARY'S SORROW TRANSFORMED INTO JOY

When we examine this final sorrow of the Blessed Virgin Mary, three stages in the transition from mourning to comfort emerge: holding on, letting go, and moving forward.

1. *Holding on*

   The first stage was learning how to hold on, and what to hold on to. In her sixth sorrow, she had held onto the broken body of her Son, but now she relinquishes his body to the tomb. What is it that Mary holds on to now?

   The song, Holding On, was written by a friend of mine who was going through a dark time in her life. Jill Swallow is a Consecrated Woman of Regnum Christi who brings out in a very beautiful way what Mary was holding onto. One line in particular strikes me: "Now I understand the cross cannot be understood but only embraced." That's a profound statement that you can make only after you have gone through sorrow and begun to experience the joy of the cross. And that is what Mary experiences. At the burial of her Son, just as she did at the Annunciation, she says, "Be it done unto me according to your will." She has to renew her "Yes" to the Father's plan, to hold on to trust in the Lord, to trust in God the father.

   Mary is holding onto what is important. Not to the secondary things, but to what truly matters: faith, hope, and love. Holding onto the three theological virtues brings rebirth where death had mangled life. They bring a resurrection which obliterates all sorrow and opens us to the fullness of what hope promises: not simply more of this life, but eternal life. What God has in store for all those who love him. Hope unlocks a new level, to new life into eternity.

2. *Letting go*

   The second stage for Mary is letting go, detachment. This is rarely easy for anyone under any circumstances. Our desire to understand what is happening, to control our life and surroundings, is strong, because it's closely tied to our sense of security and safety.

It's not easy for us to let go. Parents experience that with their kids. You want to control and protect them from every danger, any difficulty, any mistake they might make. And yet, in order for them to grow and flourish, you have to let them trip. You have to let them push the scooter and risk falling down and getting stitches in their chin. You have to let them go and play, and sometimes they will skin their knees.

I saw a little boy recently at a graduation party. Little Sebastian was full of the vigor, sense of adventure, and rambunctiousness of a two-year-old. As he ran in and out of the screen door to the grassy backyard, he would pull out first a bat and hit the wiffle ball around for a while, then run back in and grab a sword to swing at dragons and evil knights, then grab some other prop or toy. As he came in and out, he'd put his hand on the jamb, and the door would swing shut, coming close each time to smashing those little fingers. I thought, "Oh man, there is a life lesson waiting to happen right there." Sure enough, it did, Sebastian cried, got some bandaids on his fingers, and then was back out running around minutes later. For a mother, it's really hard to allow some life lessons to happen, to let go. But it's easier to let go when you know you are leaving them in the hands of God the Father, who loves your children even more than you do.

The Virgin Mary shows us that happiness doesn't consist in keeping control, but in relinquishing it to the Father. She trusts in His plan that she doesn't understand. She doesn't fully grasp it and she doesn't see everything that God has in store. But once again she says her "yes" to God's plan. She lets go, entrusting her Son to the Father. She lets go, entrusting herself to the Father, knowing he would care for her.

3. *Moving forward*

The third stage in the transition for Mary was to move forward. Humanly speaking, heavy loss and trauma tend to freeze us into inaction; we mourn, unable and unwilling to change anything. Desire seems to have abandoned us and lethargy can so easily take over.

Mary experiences these same emotions, yet she also recognizes that her Son had given her a new mission. She is now mother of John and of all Jesus's followers. She is Queen of the Apostles. She felt inadequate. She felt like she didn't have the necessary strength to move forward, but she trusted and gave her best. God worked through her to be the instrument to bring together all the Apostles after the death of our Lord. The first chapter of Acts says, "All these devoted themselves with one accord to prayer, together with some women, and Mary the mother of Jesus" (Acts 1:14). Mary became the catalyst for the joining together of the Church. She took on her new mission, she took on a new responsibility. This is crucial.

Throughout the three stages of holding on, letting go, and moving forward, the Virgin Mary probably also fostered two internal attitudes that calmed her spirit, thus helping bury her sorrow in the tomb with Jesus and then granting a foretaste of resurrection joy.

1. We can imagine how Mary paid *careful attention to the details of love*. She didn't give in to her sorrow, and say to Mary Magdalene, "Ok, you take care of his body. I am off to mourn." No, Mary was there. She took care of arranging the flowers, the oil, the perfume. Wrapping the linen shroud around his body. Placing the cloth with tender love on his face. The Blessed Mother shows us that the temptation to isolation when we mourn must be moderated with active service to others. Attentive to the little details of love, we can move beyond the pain. Joy is a fruit of love.

2. There is a second attitude that our Blessed Mother maintained through all of her sorrows: *thanksgiving*. In his life and ministry, Jesus continually gave thanks (cf. Mt 15:36, 26:27, Mark 8:6, 14:23, Luke 17:18, 22:17, John 6:11, 23). Who did he learn that from, if not his own mother? The early Christians made a habit of thanksgiving (Acts 27:35, 28:15, Rom 6:17). Where did they learn that, if not from Jesus and when gathered around the Virgin Mary in prayer? (cf. Acts 1:14) "First, I give thanks to my God through Jesus Christ," writes Paul in Romans 1:8, and similarly throughout his letters, even in

hardship. Why did he do this, if thanksgiving were not meant to be one of the key traits of a Christian?

The attitude of gratitude is a choice. It is a decision to live a life of thanksgiving, a Eucharistic life. In her insightful book, *One Thousand Gifts*, Ann Voskamp narrates how her life was transformed by the practice of *eucharisteo*, giving thanks. A simple quote from the Lutheran theologian Albert Schweitzer sparked the initial transition: "The greatest thing [in life] is to give thanks for everything. He who has learned this knows what it means to live... He has penetrated the whole mystery of life: giving thanks for everything."[73] That quote allowed her to penetrate Scripture in a new way, recognizing that thanksgiving preceded many of Jesus's miracles. It allowed her to read her own life in a new way, seeing the daily miracles in God's abundant blessings.

Thanksgiving is a question of what I choose to focus on in my life. Our natural human tendency highlights what is negative. I can harp on all my husband's defects or my wife's shortcomings, I can think about all the problems of my children and the stupid decisions they have made, I can magnify every single fault of my mother-in-law... Yes, we could do that. We can look at our own sorry lives and just get down and depressed, or we can choose to focus on what is positive, to find God's gifts that are all around us and to receive the love he puts into them.

The Virgin Mary's attitude of *eucharisteo* is depicted in a unique way in the icon on the following page.

Jesus is sitting in a chalice, in the strangest posture I have ever seen in Christian artwork. Icons don't try to perfectly portray reality, but instead try to draw out the spiritual significance behind reality. In this icon we see the infant Jesus extending his arms in blessing from the chalice, from the Eucharist. Mary is there in a quasi-priestly role, extending her arms in imitation of her Son; and in a sense presenting her Son, presenting his love, his sacrifice to the whole world for our redemption.

Mary's Eucharistic attitude of thanksgiving permeates her entire life. When I look into my own heart, do I find that same attitude in confronting the sorrows of my life?

---

73   Ann Voskamp, *One Thousand Gifts*, p. 33-34.

Unknown artist, The Unfailing Chalice Most Holy Mother of God (Neupivaemaya Chasha), 1600s, .
Original icon found in Vysotskiy Monastery in Serpukhov, Russia.

Mary isn't blind to pain, nor is she blinded by it to ignore the good. The pain and the suffering of her Son are now over. Joseph of Arimathea has come out of the woodwork and provided a tomb, an honorable burial place for her son. He was not completely rejected and abandoned; there were John and Mary Magdalene, and a few others who stayed faithful at the foot of the Cross. And his body is now in a safe place. It's not thrown out to the dogs to be ripped apart, or thrown out into the valley of Gehenna to rot. He wasn't left on the Cross for three days to be picked apart by the birds. What do I choose to focus on in my life? Do I foster an attitude of gratitude? Do I give thanks? Do I live a Eucharistic life?

The great danger of sorrow is that we become too inward looking, that we focus too much on our own misery. Mary teaches us that the way to happiness is not by focusing on our misery and closing in on self, but in opening up our heart to love. Loving, careful attention to the details of love. Letting go and holding on to what is important: faith, hope, and love; and then—through the grace of Christ, through his presence in the Eucharist—transforming our world.

THE JOY OF THE MARTYRS

The Virgin Mary's sorrows prepared her for a new mission. As a witness to Jesus's life in the most intimate way, she also is able to witness to the transformative power of the Good News. In the years after Jesus's Resurrection and Ascension into heaven, she continues to gather, form, pray with, and encourage the disciples (cf. Acts 1:14). Many of them pay the ultimate tribute of love, by laying down their own lives for Jesus. In this way, we see Mary as not only Queen of the Apostles, but also Mother of Martyrs.

The early Church Father Tertullian wrote that "the blood of martyrs is the seed of Christians."[74] Courage inspires commitment. Readiness to lose one's life reveals the sincere conviction behind belief. Endurance in the face of torture and ridicule portrays the power of the Christ and his message. The Church grows and thrives when martyrs make up "what is lacking in the afflictions of Christ on behalf of his body, which is the church." (Col 1:24)

Witnessing to Christ's love now in this life will be our greatest glory in the life to come.

Audrey Assad is a Christian songwriter and performer gifted with an extraordinary voice. She recounts the backstory to her 2016 song *Even unto Death*.

> "I have a few songs that have been songs from my gut, with all of my emotions involved, and this is one of them. I was at Matt Maher's backyard studio writing alone one day, and I came across one of the ISIS videos of beheading Christians in February 2015. There were captions in English, because they meant it for American audiences, and I got a glimpse of the martyred men. I am a Syrian-American, and my father was a refugee from Syria in the 1970s. The Arab crisis of our day is really close to my heart, and adding into that the Christian unity piece, that these men were martyred as a message to what ISIS refers to as the 'nation of the Cross'...

---

74   Tertullian, *Apologeticus*, Chapter 50.

I thought of the many martyrs around the world, but especially those in the Middle East, and wondered to myself what would be running through my head if I knew my life was about to be taken because of my faith. And so I began to write the song that became "Even Unto Death," praying for the martyrs and hoping for even a shred of their courage....

I felt a deep grief, not only for the men who were killed, but also for the killers. They were all bearers of the image of God, and I thought about how deeply tragic it was. I was weeping and weeping. All I could think was that I wanted to write a prayer that I could say if it was me on the beach about to be martyred. I saw the men praying before they were martyred. It really spoke to me, and I felt they were displaying the meekness that Jesus calls us to have and how He died on the Cross.

Philippians 2:8 says that Jesus humbled Himself, even unto death on a Cross. That was man's idea to kill Jesus that way, but God responded and said, yes, He would do that for us. I just think the martyrs display that same Spirit, and we are supposed to live that same way with our arms outstretched to the world. I wanted to grow and receive what my faith is lacking in that area."[75]

A music video of Even unto Death captures this message powerfully.[76] "The blood of martyrs is the seed of Christians."[77] This holds true even today. It gives us perspective when we look at the seventh sorrow of Mary, because each one of us in some way is called to bear witness, to be a martyr (the word "martyr" comes from the Greek word for "witness"), to carry our sorrows and turn them into the joys of Christ.

---

75   http://www.newreleasetoday.com/article.php?article_id=1697

76   https://youtu.be/aETZ6ETKAtI

77   Tertullian, Apologeticus, Chapter 50. "Sanguis Martyrum, semen Christianorum".

Wisdom is the "knowledge of divine things",[78] and is the first and the greatest of the gifts of the Holy Spirit, but often the last gift we receive. Through this final sorrow, the Virgin Mary receives the wisdom that both illumines the mind and instills an attraction to the divine. The gift of wisdom surpasses that of understanding: "The latter is a view taken by the mind, while the former is an experience undergone by the heart; one is light, the other love, and so they unite and complete one another."[79]

A wise and loving heart is the perfection of the theological virtue of charity, purified in the crucible of sorrow and suffering.

QUESTIONS FOR PERSONAL REFLECTION OR DISCUSSION:

1. What are some instances where I have learned how to let go of people, situations and control, leaving all in the hands of God the Father? How can I grow in my trust in him?

2. What things do I hold onto most tightly in my own life? Where do faith, hope, and love fit into the picture for me right now? Is there anything - e.g., my way of seeing things, my hurts, my resentment, my control - that I still need to let go of to experience the freedom Christ wants for me?

3. How could I foster more of an attitude of constant growth, of looking forward to the future, to the mission that God has in store for me? What are some ways that I can avoid letting my heart get stuck in the moment, losing perspective, drowning in my teacup of sorrow?

4. Who are the people who have helped me to detach? To hold on? To move forward? And who are the people who hold me back from being at peace in God's plan?

5. How can I help those whom I love with extra details of service?

---

78   St. Augustine, *De Trinitate xii*, 14, as quoted by St. Thomas Aquinas in the Summa Theologiae I, q.1, a.6.

79   Tanquerey, Adolphe. *The Spiritual Life*, nn. 1348-1349.

What more can I do to help them live with the type of holy detachment the Blessed Virgin Mary shows us, so that they can experience the joy that God has in store for us?

6.   In what ways do I recognize the gift of wisdom in my own life?

AN INVITATION TO PRAYER

Virgin Mary, Mother of Sorrows, but also Mother of Joy, you wrapped your Son in love before wrapping him in the Shroud. Teach me to let go and trust in the Father's plan. Show me how to hold on to faith, hope and love. Guide me on the Way—your Son—toward the life He has in store for those who love him and keep his commandments. Mary, I renew again today my trust in the Father. By following your example, guide me through sorrows to deeper joy in my life, and to the happiness of eternal life forever in heaven. Amen.

Hail Mary...

Jesus, I trust in you!

EPILOGUE

THE PATH

Seven principles form the backbone of this book.

1. Every human being desires happiness, a joy that lasts. Joy is more than a passing feeling of euphoria, a good day, fun, or contentment. It is a passion or emotion that that stems from possessing something good in the right way.[80] Ultimately, joy comes from knowing that I am loved, and loving in return. Joy is a fruit of love.

2. Because we love, we suffer. Love makes us vulnerable, opening us to disappointment, pain, and sorrow. To try to protect oneself from suffering by avoiding love leads to even greater pain, because we were made for love, and its absence brings existential anguish.

3. Suffering and sorrow without meaning, without God, lead to despair. If we suffer focused on self, we are lost in our immanence, filled with emptiness, and the pain will consume us and lead to bitterness. If we suffer with others or for others, we can discover a certain transcendence, but it is still incomplete and open to disappointment.

4. If we suffer with Christ and for Christ, we unlock the transcendence that leads to meaning, purpose, completion, and joy. It brings us to a deep level of intimacy with Christ, who chose to suffer for me.

5. Paradoxical as it may sound, suffering and sorrow are not incompatible with joy. "Joy and pain, they are but two arteries of the one heart that pumps through all those who don't numb themselves to really living."[81] Suffering and sorrow can lead to greater and deeper joy. In our human experience, we know that painful exercise can lead to health, and a discomforting operation can restore health. Through Mary's spiritual experience, we see the pathway from sorrow to joy.

---

80   If I eat a doughnut, it can offer some contentment, but if I stole it to eat it, it will turn sour in my conscience. It's not enough to have the doughnut; I have to have it in the right way.

81   Ann Voskamp, *One Thousand Gifts*, p. 84.

6. Jesus is the cause of our joy and Mary leads us to him.

7. We are free to choose the things that lead to joy—or to remain in our misery. Using our freedom wisely will lead us to choose love, always giving, always in thanksgiving. Prayer keeps us united with God. Concrete acts of love and dedication—such as a consecration of your family to the Sacred Heart of Jesus and Our Lady of Sorrows—help to solidify that daily choice to love.

OBSTACLES IN THE PATH

In each of the Virgin Mary's sorrows, we found a human experience to which we can relate. Hopefully through reflecting on them you have deepened your relationship with Jesus Christ and taken a step along the path to deeper joy.

In many ways—despite the centuries of separation—our lives are not much different from Mary's. We desire the happiness that we know can only be found in God, but encounter so many obstacles along the way. "If I just wasn't so tired in the morning, then I could pray better and I'd be holier." Or "If it weren't for that annoying person in my life, I'd be a lot more patient and kind to others." Part of the wisdom we learn from Mary's life is that *the difficulties we face are not obstacles to holiness, but are the way to it.*

Meditating on the seven sorrows of Mary has opened our hearts to this deep truth of life.

Putting that extra effort into prayer when you are tired can be an act of love more pleasing to God than hours of "perfect" piety. A smile and kind word to someone who rubs you the wrong way can sometimes be more fruitful than idyllic harmony that requires no act of virtue. "One act of thanksgiving, when things go wrong with us, is worth a thousand thanks when things are agreeable to our inclinations."[82] Obstacles give us chances to love more.

---

82   St. John of Avila, as quoted in One Thousand Gifts by Ann Voskamp, p. 79.

GIFTS OF THE JOURNEY

At times throughout these reflections, we have caught passing peeks at gifts God grants through the challenges we face in our lives. In the table below, I summarize the path we've followed on this journey to joy.

We know that from the moment of the Incarnation, the Holy Spirit overshadowed the Blessed Mother and was powerfully present in her life. More than any other person, she received the gifts of the Holy Spirit. Those gifts can be—albeit loosely—connected to each of her sorrows.

SORROW	TEMPTATION	LESSON LEARNED	GIFT OF THE H.S.
THE PROPHECY OF SIMEON	*Worry*	Live in the present Reflect on past Trust in God's Providence	*Knowledge*
THE FLIGHT INTO EGYPT	*Vanity*	Let go of human security to find it in God alone Temperance, simplicity, humility	*Understanding*
THE LOSS OF JESUS IN THE TEMPLE	*Failure*	Perfect love drives out fear Do not blame others	*Counsel*
MARY MEETS JESUS ON THE WAY TO CALVARY	*Aversion to suffering*	Encounter with Christ	*Fortitude*
JESUS DIES ON THE CROSS	*Self-pity*	"Art of accompaniment" Openness to new family, greater mission	*Fear of the Lord*
JESUS IS PIERCED WITH A LANCE AND PLACED IN MARY'S ARMS	*Despair & Bitterness*	Grieving Forgiveness	*Piety*
JESUS IS BURIED IN THE TOMB	*Separation*	Holding on Letting go Moving forward	*Wisdom*

The Catechism of the Catholic Church describes the gifts of the Holy Spirit as "permanent dispositions which make man docile in following the promptings of the Holy Spirit"[83] and they "complete and perfect the virtues of those who receive them."[84] When we follow the Holy Spirit's lead and live in him, we know that we can "do all things, through him who strengthens us" (Phil 4:13). We can overcome any obstacle, brave any danger, conquer any foe, attain the heights of holiness, and live forever. When we are filled with the Holy Spirit, nothing is impossible.

The Blessed Virgin Mary has shown us the path to this fulfillment of all our deepest desires: take up our cross and follow Jesus. Do not flee the sorrow that comes from love. By imitating Mary's virtues, learning to react to temptation and obstacles as she did, and entrusting ourselves to her motherly care, we will experience the gifts of the Holy Spirit in our lives.

---

83   Catechism of the Catholic Church, n. 1830.

84   Ibid, n. 1831.

Jean II Restout, Pentecost, 1732, Louvre Museum, Paris, France.

THE JOY OF THE JOURNEY

Just as at Pentecost, when the Holy Spirit transformed fearful men into fearless apostles, so also today an authentic outpouring of his gifts will lead us to share the Good News with others. Where there is no apostolic zeal—i.e., a joyful and confident passion to share God's love with friend and neighbor, and even total strangers—love is not yet perfected.

As we close these reflections, my hope is that your heart brims over with the love you have received, stirring that passion to evangelize. "For if we have received the love which restores meaning to our lives, how can we fail to share that love with others?"[85]

---

85   Pope Francis, *Evangelii Gaudium*, n. 8.

"There is a Marian 'style' to the Church's work of evangelization,"
and Mary is

> *a model of evangelization. We implore her maternal intercession
> that the Church may become a home for many peoples, a mother
> for all peoples, and that the way may be opened to the birth of a
> new world. It is the Risen Christ who tells us, with a power that
> fills us with confidence and unshakeable hope: "Behold, I make
> all things new" (Rev 21:5). With Mary we advance confidently
> towards the fulfilment of this promise, and to her we pray:*

> *Mary, Virgin and Mother,*
> *you who, moved by the Holy Spirit,*
> *welcomed the word of life*
> *in the depths of your humble faith:*
> *as you gave yourself completely to the Eternal One,*
> *help us to say our own "yes"*
> *to the urgent call, as pressing as ever,*
> *to proclaim the good news of Jesus.*

> *Filled with Christ's presence,*
> *you brought joy to John the Baptist,*
> *making him exult in the womb of his mother.*
> *Brimming over with joy,*
> *you sang of the great things done by God.*
> *Standing at the foot of the cross*
> *with unyielding faith,*
> *you received the joyful comfort of the resurrection,*
> *and joined the disciples in awaiting the Spirit*
> *so that the evangelizing Church might be born.*

> *Obtain for us now a new ardor born of the resurrection,*
> *that we may bring to all the Gospel of life*
> *which triumphs over death.*
> *Give us a holy courage to seek new paths,*
> *that the gift of unfading beauty*
> *may reach every man and woman.*

Virgin of listening and contemplation,
Mother of love, Bride of the eternal wedding feast,
pray for the Church, whose pure icon you are,
that she may never be closed in on herself
or lose her passion for establishing God's kingdom.

Star of the new evangelization,
help us to bear radiant witness to communion,
service, ardent and generous faith,
justice and love of the poor,
that the joy of the Gospel
may reach to the ends of the earth,
illuminating even the fringes of our world.

Mother of the living Gospel,
wellspring of happiness for God's little ones,
pray for us.
Amen. Alleluia![86]

86   Pope Francis, *Evangelii Gaudium*, n. 288.

APPENDIX
PRAYERS AND PROMISES

ROSARY OF THE SEVEN SORROWS

The Rosary of the Seven Sorrows, also known as the Chaplet of Seven
Sorrows or the Servite Rosary, is a prayer that originated with the
religious order of the Servites. In 1240, the seven founders withdrew
from the world to serve the Lord, leading a life of penance and prayer.
They introduced the rosary of the Seven Sorrows, meditating on the
principal sorrows of the Blessed Virgin Mary, and this new form of
meditative prayer was approved by several popes. In biblical usage
the number seven suggests covenant, fullness, completeness, and
abundance. The chaplet recalls seven scriptural events in which the
Blessed Virgin Mary suffered together with her divine son.

The rosary itself consists of:

> a ring of seven groups of seven beads separated by a
> small medal depicting one of the sorrows of Mary, or a
> single bead. A further series of three beads and a medal
> are also attached to the chain (before the first "sorrow")
> and these are dedicated to prayer in honor of Mary's
> tears, as well as to indicate the beginning of the chaplet.
> Conventionally the beads are of black wood or some
> other black material indicating sorrow.[87]

There is no mandatory method for praying this chaplet. The most
widespread way begins with the Sign of the Cross and an Act of
Contrition. After announcing each sorrow, a brief meditation can
be read, or a segment from the hymn *Stabat Mater Dolorosa* can be
sung or recited. An *Our Father* is prayed, followed by a *Hail Mary* on
each of the seven beads. After each set of seven, either a *Glory Be* or
a brief invocation to Our Lady of Sorrows (such as "*Sorrowful and
Immaculate Heart of Mary, pray for us!*") is prayed. The next sorrow
is then announced, and carried out in the same manner until all seven
have been meditated upon. The three Hail Marys dedicated to her tears
are prayed, and then a closing prayer is said, traditionally the following:

V. *Pray for us, O most sorrowful Virgin.*
R. *That we may be made worthy of the promises of Christ.*

87   https://en.wikipedia.org/wiki/Rosary_of_the_Seven_Sorrows

Let us pray.

Lord Jesus, we now implore, both for the present and for the hour of our death, the intercession of the most Blessed Virgin Mary, your Mother, whose holy soul was pierced at the time of your passion by a sword of grief. Grant us this favor, Savior of the world, who lives and reigns with the Father and the Holy Spirit, forever and ever. Amen.

PROMISES

It was revealed to St. Bridget of Sweden (1303–1373) that devotion to the Blessed Virgin Mary's Seven Sorrows would bring great graces. Those promises included:

1. "I will grant peace to their families."

2. "They will be enlightened about the Divine Mysteries."

3. "I will console them in their pains and I will accompany them in their work."

4. "I will give them as much as they ask for as long as it does not oppose the adorable will of my Divine Son or the sanctification of their souls."

5. "I will defend them in their spiritual battles with the infernal enemy and I will protect them at every instant of their lives."

6. "I will visibly help them at the moment of their death. They will see the face of their Mother."

7. "I have obtained this grace from my divine Son, that those who propagate this devotion to my tears and dolors, will be taken directly from this earthly life to eternal happiness since all their sins will be forgiven and my Son and I will be their eternal consolation and joy."

PRAYER OF CONSECRATION TO THE SACRED HEART OF JESUS & OUR LADY OF SORROWS[88]

I give myself and consecrate to the Sacred Heart of our Lord Jesus Christ, my person and my life, my actions, pains, and sufferings. Jesus, I desire to honor, love, and glorify your Sacred Heart with all my being. This is my purpose: to be all yours, and to do all things for the love of you. I renounce with all my heart whatever is displeasing to you. I therefore take you, O Sacred Heart, to be the only object of my love, the guardian of my life, my assurance of salvation, the remedy of my weakness and inconstancy, the atonement for all the faults of my life, and my sure refuge at the hour of death. Be then, O Heart of goodness, my justification before God the Father, and turn away from me the strokes of his righteous anger. O Heart of love, I put all my confidence in you, for I fear everything from my own wickedness and frailty, but I hope for all things from your goodness and bounty. Remove from me all that can displease you or resist your holy will; let your pure love imprint your image so deeply upon my heart, that I shall never be able to forget you or to be separated from you. May I obtain from all your loving kindness the grace of having my name written in your Heart, for in you I desire to place all my happiness and glory, living and dying united to you. Amen.

---

88   Taken in part from the prayer written by St. Margaret Mary Alacoque (1647-1690).

NOVENA PRAYER HONORING THE SEVEN SORROWS OF MARY

(Approved by Pope Pius VII in 1815)

V. *O God, come to my assistance;*
R. *O Lord, make haste to help me.*
V. *Glory be to the Father ...*
R. *As it was in the beginning ...*

1. I grieve for you, O Mary most sorrowful, in affliction of your tender heart at the prophecy of the holy and aged Simeon. O dearest Mother, by your heart so afflicted, implore for me the virtue of humility and the gift of the holy fear of God.

   Hail Mary ...

2. I grieve for you, O Mary most sorrowful, in the anguish of your most affectionate heart during the flight into Egypt and your sojourn there. O dearest Mother, by your anxious heart so troubled, obtain for me the virtue of generosity, especially toward the poor, and the gift of piety.

   Hail Mary ...

3. I grieve for you, O Mary most sorrowful, in those anxieties which tried your troubled heart at the loss of your beloved Child Jesus. O dearest Mother, by your exceedingly troubled heart implore for me the virtue of chastity and the gift of knowledge.

   Hail Mary ...

4. I grieve for you, O Mary most sorrowful, on account of the horror with which your mother-heart was stricken when meeting Jesus bearing the Cross. O dearest Mother, by your exceedingly oppressed heart implore for me the virtue of patience and the gift of fortitude.

   Hail Mary ...

5. I grieve for you, O Mary most sorrowful, on account of that martyrdom which tortured your generous heart at the death-agony of Jesus. O dearest Mother, through this thy martyred heart, implore for me the virtue of temperance and the gift of counsel.

    Hail Mary ...

6. I grieve for you, O Mary most sorrowful, in the wounding of your tender heart, by the thrust of the lance that opened the side of Jesus and pierced His most adorable Heart. O dearest Mother, by this vicarious transfixion of thy own heart, implore for me the virtue of brotherly love and the gift of understanding.

    Hail Mary ...

7. I grieve for you, O Mary most sorrowful, on account of that agony which racked your most loving heart at the burial of Jesus. O dearest Mother, through this extreme torment that filled thy burdened heart, obtain for me the virtue of zeal and the gift of wisdom.

    Hail Mary ...

    V. Sorrowful and Immaculate Heart of Mary, pray for us!
    R. That we may be made worthy of the promises of Christ.

Let us pray:

> *Let intercession be made for us, we beseech you, O Lord Jesus Christ, now and at the hour of our death, before the throne of your mercy, by the Blessed Virgin Mary, your Mother, whose most holy soul was pierced by a sword of sorrow in the hour of your bitter passion. Through you, O Jesus Christ, Savior of the world, who with the Father and the Holy Spirit lives and reigns world without end. Amen.*

STABAT MATER DOLOROSA[89]

Stabat Mater Dolorosa is considered one of the seven greatest Latin hymns of all time. It is based upon the prophecy of Simeon that a sword was to pierce the heart of His mother, Mary (Luke 2:35). The hymn originated in the 13th century during the peak of Franciscan devotion to the crucified Jesus and has been attributed to Pope Innocent III (d. 1216), St. Bonaventure (d.1274), or more commonly, Jacopone da Todi (1230–1306), who is considered by most to be the real author.

The hymn is often associated with the Stations of the Cross. In 1727 it was prescribed as a Sequence for the Mass of the Seven Sorrows of Mary (September 15) where it is still used today. In addition to this Mass, the hymn is also used for the Office of the Readings, Lauds, and Vespers for this memorial.

Stabat Mater dolorosa
iuxta Crucem lacrimosa,
dum pendebat Filius.

At the cross her station keeping, stood the mournful mother weeping, close to Jesus to the last.

Cuius animam gementem,
contristatam et dolentem
pertransivit gladius.

Through her heart, His sorrow sharing, all His bitter anguish bearing, now at length the sword has passed.

O quam tristis et afflicta fuit illa
benedicta, mater Unigeniti!

O how sad and sore distressed was that Mother, highly blest, of the sole-begotten One!

Quae maerebat et dolebat,
pia Mater, dum videbat nati
poenas inclyti.

Christ above in torment hangs, she beneath beholds the pangs of her dying glorious Son.

Quis est homo qui non fleret,
matrem Christi si videret
in tanto supplicio?

Is there one who would not weep, whelmed in miseries so deep, Christ's dear Mother to behold?

Quis non posset contristari
Christi Matrem contemplari
dolentem cum Filio?

Can the human heart refrain from partaking in her pain, in that Mother's pain untold?

---

89   From the Liturgia Horarum. Translation by Fr. Edward Caswall (1814-1878).

Pro peccatis suae gentis vidit
Iesum in tormentis,
et flagellis subditum.

Bruised, derided, cursed, defiled,
she beheld her tender Child
All with bloody scourges rent:

Vidit suum dulcem Natum
moriendo desolatum,
dum emisit spiritum.

For the sins of His own nation,
saw Him hang in desolation,
Till His spirit forth He sent.

Eia, Mater, fons amoris
me sentire vim doloris
fac, ut tecum lugeam.

O thou Mother, fount of love!
Touch my spirit from above,
make my heart with thine accord:

Fac, ut ardeat cor meum
in amando Christum Deum
ut sibi complaceam.

Make me feel as thou hast felt;
make my soul to glow and melt
with the love of Christ my Lord.

Sancta Mater, istud agas,
crucifixi fige plagas
cordi meo valide.

Holy Mother! Pierce me through,
in my heart each wound renew
of my Savior crucified:

Tui Nati vulnerati,
tam dignati pro me pati,
poenas mecum divide.

Let me share with thee His pain,
who for all my sins was slain,
who for me in torments died.

Fac me tecum pie flere,
crucifixo condolere,
donec ego vixero.

Let me mingle tears with thee,
mourning Him who mourned for me,
all the days that I may live.

Iuxta Crucem tecum stare,
et me tibi sociare
in planctu desidero.

By the Cross with thee to stay,
there with thee to weep and pray,
is all I ask of thee to give.

Virgo virginum praeclara,
mihi iam non sis amara,
fac me tecum plangere.

Virgin of all virgins blest!
Listen to my fond request:
let me share thy grief divine;

Fac, ut portem Christi mortem,
passionis fac consortem,
et plagas recolere.

Let me, to my latest breath,
in my body bear the death
of that dying Son of thine.

Fac me plagis vulnerari,
fac me Cruce inebriari,
et cruore Filii.

Wounded with His every wound,
steep my soul till it hath swooned,
in His very Blood away;

Flammis ne urar succensus,
per te, Virgo, sim defensus
in die iudicii.

Christe, cum sit hinc exire,
da per Matrem me venire
ad palmam victoriae.

Quando corpus morietur,
fac, ut animae donetur
paradisi gloria. Amen.

Be to me, O Virgin, nigh,
lest in flames I burn and die,
in His awful Judgment Day.

Christ, when Thou shalt call me hence,
by Thy Mother my defense,
by Thy Cross my victory.

While my body here decays,
may my soul Thy goodness praise,
safe in Paradise with Thee. Amen.

STABAT MATER SPECIOSA[90]

Stabat Mater Speciosa is considered one of the seven greatest Latin hymns of all time and one of the tenderest. It is based upon the Gospel account of the birth of Jesus. The hymn originated in the 13th century and has been attributed to Jacopone da Todi (1230–1306).

Stabat Mater speciosa
iuxta faenum gaudiosa,
dum iacebat parvulus.

By the crib wherein reposing,
with His eyes in slumber closing,
lay serene her Infant-boy.

Cuius animam gaudentem
laetabundam et ferventem
pertransivit iubilus.

Stood the beauteous Mother feeling
bliss that could not bear concealing,
so her face o'erflowed with joy.

O quam laeta et beata
fuit illa immaculata,
mater Unigeniti!

Oh, the rapture naught could smother
of that most Immaculate Mother
of the sole-begotten One!

Quae gaudebat et ridebat,
exultabat, cum videbat
nati partum inclyti.

When with laughing heart exulting,
she beheld her hopes resulting
In the great birth of her Son.

Quisquam est, qui non gauderet,
Christi matrem si videret
in tanto solatio?

Who would not with gratulation
see the happy consolation
of Christ's Mother undefiled?

Quis non posset collaetari,
Christi Matrem contemplari
ludentem cum Filio?

Who would not be glad surveying
Christ's dear Mother bending, praying,
playing with her heavenly Child?

Pro peccatis suae gentis
Christum vidit cum iumentis
et algori subditum.

For a sinful world's salvation,
Christ her Son's humiliation
She beheld and brooded o'er.

Vidit suum dulcem Natum
vagientem, adoratum,
vili deversorio.

Saw Him weak, a child, a stranger,
yet before Him in the manger
kings lie prostrate and adore.

90   From Latin Hymns, March, 1894. Translation by Denis Florence MacCarthy

Nato, Christo in praesepe
caeli cives canunt laete
cum immenso gaudio.

Stabat, senex cum puella
non cum verbo nec loquela
stupescentes cordibus.

Eia, Mater, fons amoris
me sentire vim ardoris
fac, ut tecum sentiam.

Fac, ut ardeat cor meum
in amatum Christum Deum
ut sibi complaceam.

Sancta Mater, istud agas,
prone introducas plagas
cordi fixas valide.

Tui Nati caelo lapsi,
iam dignati faeno nasci,
poenas mecum divide.

Fac me vere congaudere,
Iesulino cohaerere,
donec ego vixero.

In me sistat ardor tui,
puerino fac me frui
dum sum in exilio.

Virgo virginum praeclara,
mihi iam non sis amara,
fac me parvum rapere.

Fac, ut pulchrum infantem portem,
qui nascendo vicit mortem,
volens vitam tradere.

O'er that lowly manger winging,
joyful hosts from heaven were singing
canticles of holy praise.

While the old man and the maiden,
speaking naught, with hearts o'erladen,
pondered on God's wondrous ways.

Fount of love, forever flowing,
with a burning ardor glowing,
make me, Mother, feel like thee.

Let my heart, with graces gifted
all on fire, to Christ be lifted,
and by Him accepted be.

Holy Mother, deign to bless me,
with His sacred Wounds impress me,
let them in my heart abide.

Since He came, thy Son, the Holy,
to a birthplace, ah, so lowly,
all His pains with me divide.

Make me with true joy delighted,
to Child-Jesus be united
while my days of life endure.

While an exile here sojourning,
make my heart like thine be burning
with a love divine and pure.

Spotless Maid and sinless Woman,
make us feel a fire in common,
make my heart's long longing sure.

Virgin of all virgins highest,
prayer to thee thou ne'er denyest,
let me bear thy sweet Child too.

Let me bear Him in my bosom,
Lord of life, and never lose Him,
since His birth doth death subdue.

Fac me tecum satiari,
Nato me inebriari,
stantem in tripudio.

Let me show forth how immense is
the effect on all my senses
of an union so divine.

All who in the crib revere Him,
like the shepherds watching near Him,
will attend Him through the night.

Inflammatus et accensus,
obstupescit omnis sensus
tali me commercio.

By thy powerful prayers protected,
grant, O Queen, that His elected
may behold heaven's moving light.

Fac, me Nato custodiri,
verbo Dei praemuniri
conservari gratia.

Make me by His birth be guarded,
by God's holy word be warded,
by His grace till all is done.

Quando corpus morietur,
fac, ut animae donetur
tui nati gloria. Amen.

When my body lies obstructed,
make my soul to be conducted,
to the vision of thy Son. Amen.

LITANY OF THE SACRED HEART OF JESUS

In 1899, Pope Leo XIII approved the Latin version of the Litany of the Sacred Heart of Jesus for public use. It was a synthesis of prior versions, and varied translations of the litany exist.[91]

> V. Lord, have mercy on us.
> R. Christ, have mercy on us.
> V. Lord, have mercy on us. Christ, hear us.
> R. Christ, graciously hear us.
> V. God the Father of Heaven, have mercy on us.

God the Son, Redeemer of the world,   R. have mercy on us.

> God the Holy Spirit,
> Holy Trinity, one God,
> Heart of Jesus, Son of the Eternal Father,
> Heart of Jesus, formed by the Holy Spirit in the Virgin Mother's womb,
> Heart of Jesus, substantially united to the Word of God,
> Heart of Jesus, of infinite majesty,
> Heart of Jesus, holy temple of God,
> Heart of Jesus, tabernacle of the Most High,
> Heart of Jesus, house of God and gate of heaven,
> Heart of Jesus, glowing furnace of charity,
> Heart of Jesus, vessel of justice and love,
> Heart of Jesus, full of goodness and love,
> Heart of Jesus, abyss of all virtues,
> Heart of Jesus, most worthy of all praise,
> Heart of Jesus, King and center of all hearts,
> Heart of Jesus, in whom are all the treasures of wisdom and knowledge,
> Heart of Jesus, in whom dwells all the fullness of the Godhead,
> Heart of Jesus, in whom the Father was well pleased,
> Heart of Jesus, of whose fullness we have all received,
> Heart of Jesus, desire of the everlasting hills,

91 See for example http://www.usccb.org/prayer-and-worship/prayers-and-devotions/litanies/litany-of-the-sacred-heart-of-jesus.cfm and https://www.ewtn.com/devotionals/litanies/sacred_heart.htm.

Heart of Jesus, patient and rich in mercy,
Heart of Jesus, rich to all who call upon you,
Heart of Jesus, fount of life and holiness,
Heart of Jesus, propitiation for our offenses,
Heart of Jesus, overwhelmed with reproaches,
Heart of Jesus, bruised for our iniquities,
Heart of Jesus, obedient even unto death,
Heart of Jesus, pierced with a lance,
Heart of Jesus, source of all consolation,
Heart of Jesus, our life and resurrection,
Heart of Jesus, our peace and reconciliation,
Heart of Jesus, victim for our sins,
Heart of Jesus, salvation of those who hope in you,
Heart of Jesus, hope of those who die in you,
Heart of Jesus, delight of all saints,

V. Lamb of God, who takes away the sins of the world,
R. spare us, O Lord.
V. Lamb of God, who takes away the sins of the world,
R. graciously hear us, O Lord.
V. Lamb of God, who takes away the sins of the world,
R. have mercy on us.
V. Jesus, gentle and humble of heart,
R. Make my heart more like yours.

Let us pray.

Almighty and eternal God, look upon the Heart of your most beloved
Son and upon the praises and satisfaction which he offers you in the
name of sinners; and to those who implore your mercy, in your great
goodness, grant forgiveness in the name of the same Jesus Christ, your
Son, who lives and reigns with you forever and ever. Amen.

Made in the USA
Columbia, SC
08 April 2020

91034094R00102